THREE TIMES
I PLEADED

GOD'S TRANSFORMING POWER THROUGH
PAIN AND DISAPPOINTMENT

MICHAEL CRANFORD

Published in Dana Point, California by Days Fly, LLC.

ISBN 978-1-7325718-0-8 (ebook)
ISBN 978-1-7325718-1-5 (soft cover)
ISBN 978-1-7325718-2-2 (audio)

CONTENTS

THREE TIMES I PLEADED

Introduction:

Crossroads of Decision

What is the big picture behind the hardship, loss, and suffering we experience in life? The problem is that we often can't see the big picture. All we can see are the circumstances immediately around us. When our plans fail, and we experience pain and disappointment,

- We feel alone.
- We feel like failures.
- We feel like nothing really matters, that it's all meaningless.
- We feel like we don't deserve anything good, so we don't expect things to work out.

This is the experience of someone who doesn't feel loved. We've all been there. I've been there. I've had all these feelings, and I've questioned God's goodness in allowing me to go through difficult times. *If you really love me, God, why am I going through this? Does my life matter to you? Are you listening to me?*

If you don't feel loved, you take risks. You can find yourself drawn into self-destructive behavior. You might try to control people and circumstances out of a desperate need to change things. You can quickly spring from a life-shattering disappointment to a chain of bad decisions that make the situation even worse. We sometimes look for solace from our pain in unhealthy relationships or addictive patterns. We scramble to find anything that can fill our emptiness and help us forget the people and circumstances that caused us so much heartache.

For followers of Jesus Christ, pain and disappointment put us at a crossroads. Will we trust God, or not? Will we place our cares in his hands, or will we try to find a solution under our own power?

We live in a world filled with people who are desperate to know that someone loves them. That they are valuable. That they are not alone. That someone waits, no matter what happens in this life, with open arms. Someone does wait for you with open arms, no matter the circumstances of your life, your disappointment, or your failures. You need to picture him—the one who waits for you. That vision drives us to choose his way when we experience pain and reach that crossroads. If we do, we will find ourselves lifted up by an inexplicable working of his power. For many of us, hardship is an essential step for the Holy Spirit to take command and use us to accomplish his plan. His plan is personal, transformative, and miraculous. He longs to share it with us.

Difficult Life Situations that Hold Us in Their Grip

All hardship is not the same, though. When pain and loss strike us, they can take many different forms. Personal forms of tragedy, like the loss of a spouse or child, impact us differently than having someone intentionally hurt us. If we've played a part in the loss we're experiencing, it's different and can be worse than something entirely out of our control. The guilt can be overwhelming. If we've had similar experiences of pain from earlier times in our life, a new failure or loss can cause us to relive those memories and overwhelm us in a way that other people may not appreciate.

Life is filled with difficulties, but some have a grip on us so strong we almost can't let them go. They grab hold of our thoughts and control our behavior. In managing the pain they cause, we might seek help from a source other than God and eventually find ourselves even more hopeless and desperate than when we started. We need a solution so that, when they arrive, we are prepared and don't lose hope. Thinking we're immune is only going to make it harder when disaster strikes. If we haven't lived through these kinds of hardships, we need to recognize and accept the fact that difficulties lie ahead for each of us. The world around us makes it inevitable. Those difficulties can include:

- Breakup
- Divorce
- Loss of a job
- Natural disaster
- Loss of a home, finances, or possessions
- Failure in a life-goal
- Loss of a pregnancy
- Old age and a lack of support
- Medical problems
- Loss of a loved one, such as a spouse or family member

Sometimes it's not a specific event but the piling up of smaller losses over time that causes us to lose hope that things can be better. We might have the experience of being overwhelmed by a business failure, an interpersonal conflict, a legal challenge, or a traffic accident. We all struggle at times with disappointment, loss of self-esteem, and anxiety as a result of circumstances when things take a wrong turn. The emotions we experience are part of being human, and disaster is part of the world we live in. It has been this way from the beginning.

Different Kinds of Pain but the Same Questions

The early Christians faced many difficulties. They were poorly treated by Jewish groups (John 16:1-2; Acts 14:2; 17:5) and the pagan government alike (John 15:18-20; Rom. 8:35-37; 1 Pet. 4:12-16). They were struggling with meeting their basic needs in a political system which didn't favor the ordinary citizen and left most people in poverty (see Luke 4:18; Gal. 2:10). Some people in the early church, having come to Christ, were being abandoned by their pagan spouses, or were being mistreated by their pagan spouses to the point they wanted to leave their marriages (1 Cor. 7:10-16). Within a decade following Paul's letter to the church in Rome, encouraging them in their suffering (Rom. 8:18), the Emperor Nero's persecution of Christians resulted in widespread suffering, torture, and death.

The fact that their difficulties and temptations are not necessarily the same as ours doesn't change the underlying feelings of abandonment, pain, and despair that we all share in times of crisis. The same questions arose in their minds as ours, the same uncertainty about the love of God and his plans for their future. They faced the same decision we do today when our dreams don't come true, or we suffer the loss of something or someone we hold dear: *Will we trust God? Will we look to him as our source of strength?*

Much of the spread of early Christianity was the

fruit of one man's labor. This man faced hardship and opposition at every step—from detractors, civil authorities, and natural calamity. Ironically, he was a highly-esteemed Jewish leader who brought hardship to others before his conversion. Through the circumstances this man faced, God revealed his plan of salvation to the people of that time who walked in darkness and had nowhere to turn. They were a lot like you and me, with their own dreams and hopes. In their own turn, they faced difficulties and hardship. The Apostle Paul was not only the one who brought them the good news of salvation by faith in Christ, he also offered them hope and encouragement along the journey of faith he demonstrated through his own suffering.

Paul offers them—and us—the key to understanding the purpose of suffering in the lives of believers. It is not merely an insight given to him by the Holy Spirit; it is an insight that came from his own pain and hardship.

Five times I received from the Jews the forty lashes minus one. Three times I was beaten with rods, once I was pelted with stones, three times I was shipwrecked, I spent a night and a day in the open sea, I have been constantly on the move. I have been in danger from rivers, in danger from bandits, in danger from my fellow Jews, in danger from Gentiles; in danger in the city, in danger in the country, in danger at sea; and in danger from false believers. I have labored and toiled and have often gone without sleep; I have known hunger and thirst and have often gone without food; I have been cold and naked. (2 Cor. 11:24-27)

Paul couldn't have written the passage that immediately follows this one—a passage that explains the purpose in suffering—apart from these circumstances. There was something he learned in the process—a secret. That secret is not obvious, and it eludes us in the moments we need it most. In it is the solution to all our pain, the answer to our despair. It marks the beginning of a transformation that the Holy Spirit will do within us through hardship; it is the key to experiencing his power in the center of our lives. We can learn the secret also, but only through the difficulties that we face, and only if we trust him.

Choosing Transformation

When we reach the crossroads of decision in times of suffering, we may not fully understand the choice that is in front of us. What do we do with our pain and loss? We might think our choice is either to endure pain or find an escape. If we don't fight back, we're afraid we might be steamrolled by life. As Christians, we might consider it to be little more than the choice to sin or keep our impulses in check. The real choice is something even more profound. It is not simply about feeling better; it's an opportunity. We have the option to gain from a situation that we may only see as a loss.

The choice we face is whether we want to experience the transforming power of the Holy Spirit.

What I'm describing is a different way of looking at hardship and difficulties. They are a critical step on the way to becoming the people we are meant to be and having the life we are meant to have. We can choose to view them in terms of what we have lost and try desperately to fill the void, or we can look at them as a chance to submit to the Lord and have him work through us. When we do—*if* we do—our circumstances may or may not change, but *we* do. Suffering is the way God transforms us to accomplish his purposes on this earth. Pain and loss are the keys to experiencing his power. That power is a miracle in a world filled with the ordinary.

In a culture of personal gratification, we resist the idea. Everything in us struggles against it. We are drawn to the ordinary and familiar. We cannot choose whether or not we will go through hardship, but we can decide if we will allow the Lord to change us through it.

We don't automatically desire change in our lives; it requires that we give things up. It's much easier to continue along the path we've been traveling than react differently. Change implies we've been doing things wrong, and that can be difficult to admit. We become comfortable with our lives—the familiar frustrations, sins, and habits. We keep repeating the same mistakes, caught up in our daily routine and doubting that our lives really matter. We might come to believe we don't deserve anything more than what we already have, and settle for ordinary lives that make little difference in light of eternity. This mindset can lead us to waste our years on earth. Hardship may be the only thing that gives us the chance to become everything God wants us to be.

This book explores the biblical teaching of how God uses difficulties in our lives to change us and make us people through whom he can reveal his power. We will journey through the misconceptions that cause us to miss the purpose in our suffering and reject the work that God intends to do in us as we trust him through hardship and disappointment. We live in a culture and a time when we're less willing than ever to accept that losses can lead to blessings and that God uses adversity to change us in ways that are essential for his work. As a consequence, we see very little of God's power in our lives or in the church. But each of us has the potential to let the Spirit work in and through the difficulties we face to change us and reflect his power in ways we can scarcely dream of, and produce an outworking of joy and peace that will carry us through the greatest of difficulties without fear. This book is intended to unravel God's plan and your potential to have that kind of life.

I'm a stubborn man. I put my trust in Christ when I was young, but over the years I had my own plans to make my dreams come true. I decided that my plans for happiness must be his plans for me also. Sometimes it worked out, but more often it didn't. I was missing something important. The problem was not the difficulties and disappointment I faced, over and over, but the man experiencing them. I finally reached a moment when I prayed and asked God to remove anything in my life that was preventing him from using me. That prayer was answered, but not in a way I'd have expected. The next steps on my journey led to hardship, and I began to struggle and pull back. In his mercy, God put me in a situation where I could no longer control the circumstances that were hurting me. I was at a crossroads. Following Christ is never easy, but after a time I could see my way to the goal, and I committed myself to the path of his choosing.

God has a plan and purpose to change you and empower you to accomplish great things. He wants you to reject an ordinary life and pursue one filled with joy, peace, power, and miracle. To put your feet on that path means difficulties, but the road leads past them and on to a destiny beyond anything this world can offer. He calls you to that destiny, and he waits there for you, with open arms.

The words in this book are intended for those who have chosen to follow Christ. His transforming power is available to anyone who has put their trust in him. If you do not already know him, you are at a crossroads of a different sort. My prayer is that you would set your feet on his path. If you turn to the appendix, you will find more information about the new life that awaits you.

Chapter 1:
A Shift in Perspective

The way you look at something can change every-thing. In C. S. Lewis's *The Lion, the Witch and the Wardrobe*, there is a moment it seems like everything has gone horribly wrong. Aslan, the great lion, is bru-tally killed by the White Witch. Evil has apparently triumphed over good. The children who have trav-eled to Narnia and come to love Aslan are left deject-ed and in despair. We are too, as we follow the story, assuming we don't already know how it ends. When Aslan's apparent defeat is revealed as the very thing needed to secure victory, the suffering that led to the outcome is no longer tragic. Sorrow turns into joy. The pain he experienced is washed away by the good that came from it. Sometimes all we need is a change in perspective.

It's the same in our lives. When we face difficulties, pain, and hardship, we typically can't see a purpose. We become overwhelmed by loss and disappointment and can't find the perspective needed to feel differently about what is happening. The idea that our difficulties could be the very thing we need to achieve victory escapes us. This may be, in part, because we can't picture what that victory could be. It is difficult to see beyond our circumstances and to have hope.

One thing I've learned is that I gain a broader perspective over time. When I look back on my failure, hardship, and circumstances in earlier phases of my life, I perceive them differently than when I was going through them. Situations that once left me anxious and desperate now have no influence over me. The times when I didn't have enough money to cover my bills are erased in the blessings of later years. In the span of time, free from the circumstances that cause us so much pain, our perspective will change. The challenge that confronts us is what to do in the present. *How do I make sense of what I am going through? How can I feel better?* We need to rest ourselves in God's hands and allow him to prove faithful in his own timing. But the world that surrounds us looks at this differently, and we are drawn to its way of thinking.

The Culture of Happiness

Trusting God through hardship is difficult in our culture. We are encouraged to live for the moment, not for eternity. If we are seeking instant gratification and happiness, we will not persevere through suffering and become the people we were meant to be. We will instead find ourselves drawn into even greater emptiness and despair.

It's not the image that Hollywood paints for us. What we desperately long for, and what they portray, is a fairy tale. It is a predictable formula that leads to box office success. It is the story of attractive people who find love, power, material wealth, and fame in a never-ending pursuit of individual happiness and instant gratification. Movies which break the mold often receive critical acclaim but make a lot less money. We're hard-wired to want the vision of life that the media depicts for us in such vivid terms. The world around us is in rapid pursuit of it. We believe we will be happy if we can be like the characters and celebrities we idolize. We want what they have.

I've found myself caught up in this way of thinking, desperate to find happiness when things fall apart around me. I've chosen the quick way out rather than trust God's timing. Part of my confusion in those moments was losing track of why I am here in the first place—what God's purposes were in my life. It's easy to get confused in the culture we live in. We are captivated by dreams of personal success and happiness. We want the same fate, romance, happiness, wealth, and freedom from responsibility as the characters in our favorite shows. We have difficulty envisioning a life where these pursuits are not necessarily God's plan for us. Because we can't picture something greater than the temporary happiness everyone else is after, we begin to regard God as our helper—someone who exists to make our lives better. We convince ourselves that our plan for happiness is the same as his will. If things don't go the way we hoped, we become confused and bitter. We try to control circumstances and people, to make sure we end up with the result we need.

It's a cycle we are all drawn to, seeking a way out of our pain at any cost. We pursue the quickest path to the happiness we believe is our highest goal. In the process, we lose our way and set ourselves up for crushing disappointment. There is no way to escape the actual pain of loss, but our lack of vision can trap us in a downward spiral of even more significant damage and disappointment. Instead of trusting God and seeking his purposes in our pain, we miss out on his blessings and create new problems for ourselves. The world around us falls into despair under the guile of temporary happiness. Celebrities who seem to have it all nonetheless fall into drug addiction, divorce, and suicide.

Pursuing the fulfillment that comes from setting our feet on Jesus's path allows us to make sense of pain and hardship. We can find strength and victory in knowing that our pain and disappointment do not mean his plan for our lives has gone wrong. If we set our sights on his dreams and purposes, we can experience fulfillment no matter what life throws our way. We may not always have happiness, but we can have joy. Joy is the experience that the world around us desperately craves but cannot realize apart from Jesus Christ. We need to reject any substitute. There is nothing more powerful than what the Lord does in and through us when we put our trust in him. It is transforming. It will allow us to come through any difficulty with peace. The world's substitutes all come to an end, but what the Lord offers us lasts forever.

Caught Up in the Moment

I've had my bumper mashed in the same supermarket parking lot by two different people in the same year. Both were backing up their cars and hit me while I had the brake on. One was in a hurry to leave, the other was angry at another vehicle blocking them. Neither checked their rearview mirror. My kids were in the car both times and were shaken up by the experience.

I don't park in that cramped lot anymore; I leave my car across the street and walk over to the supermarket. I do it more for the sake of my kids than anything; my car isn't going to be around forever. One extra scratch or ding doesn't bother me. That's one of the great things about driving a used car, and one of the reasons people feel more relaxed about a new car once it gets a few bumps and scratches. You can picture the day when the car is going to be gone, and it changes your values in the present. You don't value things the same way once you recognize they're temporary. What really matters are things that last.

You can look at an old car, knowing it is destined for the scrapyard, and adjust your values accordingly. Looking at the treasures and pursuits of your life that way is more difficult. The people you love, the home you saved for, the marriage you cherish—these are the things we value the most, and in many cases, our identity is interconnected with them. Losing a spouse or a child can not only devastate us emotionally but leave us without a sense of purpose or value. The hardship that follows massive financial loss can leave us anxious and depressed but also cause us to wonder about all the years we worked so hard and saved so carefully.

Knowing the end of a thing changes the way you look at it in the present. It's true of the things we own, and it's true of the things we invest our time in. The difficulty is when you can't envision the end of something or choose not to do so. This can apply to relationships, possessions, or your bodily health. If we view these things as if they are permanent and essential to our happiness, we can be devastated by their loss. We set ourselves up for a moment of overwhelming despair. If we invest our lives in possessions and pursuits that don't have eternal value, we can make it even worse. We not only lose the thing itself but also the time, emotion, and resources that could have been spent on something more meaningful.

What I am suggesting is not to care less about pursuits and possessions that must eventually pass away but to recognize that they will. With that realization, our hearts will change. The certainty that things are temporary—and that includes our health, our income, and even the commitments people make to us—leads us to find our identity in things that can never be taken from us. We can't avoid heartache and disappointment but we can achieve joy, peace, and the transforming presence of God in the middle of our difficulties, no matter how extreme. If we have invested in eternal things, our hearts will remain focused on what cannot be lost, and we can continue on.

> *"Do not store up for yourselves treasures on earth, where moths and vermin destroy, and where thieves break in and steal. But store up for yourselves treasures in heaven, where moths and vermin do not destroy, and where thieves do not break in and steal. For where your treasure is, there your heart will be also." Matt. 6:19-21*

This passage is frequently used in support of tithing, but the intended application is much broader. Jesus isn't just saying we should give money to God rather than spend frivolously. He is telling us where our hearts should be. If our hearts are fixed on eternal things, they are not wrapped up in what is temporary. They can sustain any loss. These are the hearts we are meant to have. They are the same as his heart. Our hearts become like his by investing in treasures that last forever.

The first step in doing that is to take an assessment of the things in our lives that control us. We can begin by identifying the things that demand our time, money, and passion, and considering if we're willing to let them go. If you can give something up, you know it isn't controlling you. If you are being controlled, or you think you might be, the best way to become free is to do just that—get rid of it. Looking at something and thinking, *This isn't important to me,* may not be enough if you continue to let that thing dominate your thoughts and time. The goal is to look at *all* your material belongings this way—as things that are unessential to becoming the person you are meant to be and letting them go in favor of things that matter. The more you do, the freer you are.

Jesus's value is to look at things that are temporary as they truly are. We will lose those things in the passage of time. We can find peace in those moments if our eyes are fixed on the greater treasures that lie ahead. The goals and pursuits of your life are never certain and are ultimately out of your control, but no one can stop the plans that God has for you in eternity.

Sometimes, the way to gain Jesus's value is to have everything taken from you and allow the Lord to draw you into the riches of his love. Sometimes, the way to get there is to take small steps in trusting him and investing in his kingdom—small steps that lead to large ones. What I can tell you is that if you allow your perspective to change, your heart will change. This is Jesus's principle, for giving and for everything else. When your heart changes, you will long for the things he values. The vision of what lies ahead will control you far more than the temporary distractions that hold you back. You will understand why men and women have given their lives rather than deny their Savior. It will all make sense, and it will be your heart also. With that heart, you will find fulfillment and joy no matter what this life brings. And one day, the things you invested in will be there waiting for you.

Getting What We Ask For

There is a popular book series that depicts prayer as a way to strengthen angels in their battle against demons. As people pray, the angels literally become empowered, as if prayer itself were the necessary ingredient for an angel's strength. I remember reading it many years ago, and it did prompt me to get on my knees. As I was praying, I was picturing the angels growing bigger and tougher. I didn't want feeble angels guarding me.

The only problem is that this reduces prayer to magic. It makes the prayer itself seem powerful, not God. At one time, I had this conception of prayer— that it was about asking for something when I'm in trouble and all my efforts to fix things have ended in failure. I'd say some words and cross my fingers. Maybe things would work out, but more often they didn't.

One of the reasons why we think about prayer this way is that we live in a culture that conditions us to get our needs met as quickly as we can, in whatever way presents itself to us at the moment. This reaction is what drives advertising; if it didn't work, we wouldn't buy the products and experiences marketed to us, and the system would fall apart. We are told that having lots of choices is the greatest possible good and that if someone is limiting your choices, you're not really free to pick what is best for you. When we have a need, we turn to God with the same expectation, that he will meet our needs the way we want and in the timeframe we specify. Prayer becomes no more than that, for most of us—the moment we go to God to get something. If he doesn't give us what we ask for, we feel like he's deliberately blocking us from being happy.

I went through a disappointing series of events in my life and approached prayer this way—as a means to get the thing I wanted. I asked God to change the circumstances that were hurting me. When I didn't get the answer I wanted, I began to grow bitter. *If you are real,* I thought, *why don't you show yourself?* If prayer is about getting something from God and things don't work out the way that you want, it leaves you with the impression that he's too busy to care. It may cause you to wonder if he's there at all.

That's not prayer. Not really. Prayer is the deepest work of the human spirit, and it's not about manipulating God to do what we want. It's not magic. Prayer is the place where we agree with God's purposes. It is a moment when we set aside the things that are distracting us and bow before him. It starts with submission to his sovereignty and acknowledgment of who he is. It means being willing to set aside what you want, if it is not his will.

Paul struggled with a burden, perhaps a medical problem, which he refers to as his "thorn in the flesh" (2 Cor. 12:7). We can't know for certain what he was referring to, but he describes his experience of it as torment. He pleaded with God three times to remove it from him. God's answer to him was, *No*. There was a greater purpose in Paul's suffering. The purpose behind it was God's, though, not Paul's. Not initially, anyway. Something changed as a result of Paul's prayer. We can see the results of it in his ministry and his writings. What changed was his heart. He yearned for and accepted God's will, however difficult, and however contrary to his immediate needs. The result in his life was God's power. We can experience the same result, if we agree with God's purposes and remain faithful through suffering and loss.

Avoiding pain is a natural response. We tend to interpret God's will in terms of escaping our pain. We often approach our pain and loss with the assumption that God's will for us is the thing that will make us feel better. We pray to God about a course of action we intend to take with or without his help, rather than submit to a process that might change us and set us free. If we do, we are missing the true role of prayer in our lives.

Our suffering and heartache at times seem unbearable. Prayer may be offered at those desperate moments, but it is always with the understanding that God knows what is best. You don't always get what you ask for. You are told to bring your petition before him, but more importantly, to submit to his will. It may not be what you want. If that's the case, you are the one who needs to change. You need to trust your Father. You do that by praying that his will be done. If you do, you *will* change. You will long for the things he wants. And you will find that your prayers will be answered.

The Pattern That Surrounds

We are creatures of habit. When I was a teenager, I could crack my knuckles loudly. It was a nervous habit, and I couldn't keep myself from doing it. Over the years I've picked up different habits, many of a positive sort. Expressing appreciation for people's help is one of those. Another is having consideration for the feelings of others. I didn't have those habits back when I was cracking my knuckles, and fortunately, I lost the knuckle-cracking when I got older. I'd call that a good trade-off.

Habits develop from behavior. You can develop a habit for nearly anything if you do it enough. The habit doesn't reside in your actions, though; it happens in your mind. The way you think gradually adapts to support the things you do. Your values change to match your behavior. Then, in turn, your actions influence your values. If your habit is exercise, for example, this metamorphosis is a good thing. Making time for exercise will lead to habits that increasingly motivate you to exercise. If your habit is using profanity, though, it may not work out so well.

The more you use vulgar language, the less likely you are to pay attention to what you're saying or the way others receive it.

To find purpose in suffering, we need to reject the perspective of culture. We need to stand in opposition to the tendency to dull our pain at any cost. We need to find the courage to trust God and put our anxiety into his hands. We need to persevere and live holy lives, even when we're unhappy and things aren't going well. The problem is that we're being trained to find the shortest path to the least pain, to pursue comfort and not character. We're being led from the difficult but meaningful path that Jesus laid out to a broader road that promises fewer difficulties and more creature comforts. That path tells us to waste our time on things that don't matter, to get drunk or find happiness in meaningless sexual relationships.

We adopt the perspective of our culture because we have adopted its behaviors. We live out the world's priorities because we have internalized its values. The way to break free from the perspectives we have been discussing is to live differently. If we live differently, we will think differently. Paul explains this in the closing section of Romans:

> *Therefore, I urge you, brothers and sisters, in view of God's mercy, to offer your bodies as a living sacrifice, holy and pleasing to God—this is your true and proper worship. Do not conform to the pattern of this world, but be transformed by the renewing of your mind. Then you will be able to test*

and approve what God's will is—his good, pleasing and perfect will. (Rom. 12:1-2)

In v. 2 he tells them not to conform to the pattern of the world, but to be transformed by the renewing of their minds. The way they get there is by doing what he says in v. 1: they must offer their bodies as living sacrifices, holy and pleasing to God. If we live with the goal of pleasing God and not the world around us, our thinking will change. We can break free from the world's way of thinking if we live differently than the world around us. It's like breaking any bad habit; the patterns have become so ingrained that we almost aren't aware of them. To think differently we must live differently. If we live differently, we will change. We experience transformation if we don't conform to the pattern that surrounds us. The consequence is not merely that we follow God's will, but that it becomes tested and proven through our lives (Rom. 12:2). God's will for us isn't just an idea; it's a reality that is demonstrated by the way we live.

We are surrounded by values; the media bombards us with them. We are told what matters, how we should live, what our goals should be. These values permeate every area of our lives. Unless we live in a Christian bubble (e.g., work at a church, attend a Christian university, and cancel our cable subscriptions), the tendencies, habits, and beliefs of the world we live in become impressed on us. It's like diving deep beneath the surface of a lake; you can hold your breath for a while, but it is difficult not to take some water in.

As with a tendency to use profanity, we find ourselves adopting the habits everyone else does. We act like everyone else, getting excited about the same things, pursuing the same goals. We are amused by the same raunchy programming, the same sense-dulling addictions, and the same time-wasting diversions.

The problem is that the vision of life that captivates almost everyone in this world is not Christ's. To the degree that we become drawn to the world around us, we distance ourselves more and more from the heart of the one who called us to something greater (see James 4:4). We don't learn from difficulties in life, and we end up trapped, repeating the same patterns of failure, over and over, just like everyone else. We are more likely to fall into this behavior at times when we experience hardship and suffering.

We're stuck in habits from overexposure to worldly values. The church today, as a whole, looks a lot more like media's framing of American culture than it does the first group of men and women who gave their lives for Christ. We are not just disconnected from them in our values; we are disconnected in our approach to following Jesus. Christ called men and women to leave their old lives behind and follow in his steps. This isn't happening if our new lives are fundamentally the same as our old ones.

The way we break out of the misconception that happiness comes from immediate gratification is by choosing not to gratify ourselves that way. You need to isolate the thing you are doing to make yourself feel better rather than trusting God, and then not do it. If you can envision that what you are doing is hurting you, you can stop it. Whether it's frivolous spending, drinking, pornography, or a relationship you shouldn't be in. If you can separate yourself from the habit for a period of time, it will loosen its grip, and your thinking will change.

When we experience loss or hardship, our first response should be to seek God in prayer. Not just to bring him our request for assistance, but to make sure we aren't holding onto sin or resentment that might interfere with drawing close to him and hearing his voice. Our second response should be to pursue holiness. We should behave as his children as we wait for his purposes in our suffering. If you've been struggling with sin, there is no better time to make things right than when pain and hardship strike. We show God that, no matter how far off we've been, we have our eyes firmly on him. Our obedience is an affirmation of our trust. As we wait for him to reveal his power in the middle of our difficulties, we do so as people who are committed to his values. It's the only way we can truly show him that we trust him and are listening.

God isn't far away when we need his help, but our sin interferes with his ability to bless us. He can't bless what isn't right. He can sustain our lives even when we're disobedient, but we're usually looking for more than our daily bread when our world falls apart. We are looking for his presence like never before. We yearn to see a miracle in the middle of our pain. Our holiness communicates to him that we know he is holy and has no tolerance for sin. We take on his values so that we can receive his blessing and power. The life we have in Christ comes in spite of our mistakes, but God's power only works in us and through us to the degree we set things right in our lives and walk with him. By walking in holiness, we create an opportunity for him to glorify himself through our situation.

The One Who Waits With Open Arms

Any race or journey requires that you know the destination to which you are heading. Without a destination, you wouldn't know where to go. It is essential for any journey, and there is no journey more important than the journey of your life. Our destination is that moment we will cross the finish line and win the prize. The prize is not so much what we will win as it is the one who waits for us there. The moment we step across the finish line and into his arms, the burdens we have carried in this life will have no weight at all.

The world has a different approach to pain and difficulties because it has a different destination. Paul writes, "If the dead are not raised, 'Let us eat and drink, for tomorrow we die'" (1 Cor. 15:32). We are surrounded by opportunities to live out this perspective. If death is really the end, then there is no greater purpose than to grab whatever happiness you can before it's too late. In that case, the end is not so much a destination as an expiration date. It's like that carton of milk you left in the refrigerator too long. It is a finish—but not for a purpose. In this view, all purposes end at death. The only meaning you have in life is what satisfaction you have along the way. We get drawn into the behaviors associated with this perspective because the destination seems a long way off and the journey is difficult. We want a rest from the pain and difficulties of life, and the world offers that in abundance.

You've probably been in a race at some point. A race requires endurance—that you keep up the pace and not stop for unnecessary breaks. There are times when the pain is so intense that you want to stop, but doing so would render your efforts to that point meaningless. A race also requires focus; you have to pay attention to what you're doing or else risk being taken out by an obstacle or distraction. If we choose to view hardships as expected parts of the race we are in, as followers of Christ, we can find the strength to persevere through them. What's the worst that can happen? If the tragedy we face is so great that it costs us our very lives, we have peace in knowing that we have reached the finish line and will receive the prize we were promised. The end of our hardship and pain is the finish line. That vision empowered Paul. It can do the same for us.

Not all suffering is directly related to ministry, but our ministry does flow from the difficulties we face in life. Those difficulties can cause us to draw closer to God and seek him, or they can cause us to pull away and find a solution to our pain elsewhere. Our victory becomes part of the message we share about God's faithfulness with others. If you think in these terms, then all suffering is related in some way to living for Christ. The question is whether we will use it to propel us into action or if we will turn in some other direction. Everything in the world tries to pull us off course. The way we should react is to use our hardship to draw close to God and let him use us more powerfully.

When you're in a long-distance race, you are not likely to get distracted. Sheer physical exhaustion will continually remind you that the finish line is somewhere ahead. But when you're walking, your mind can drift, and you can find yourself lost or tripping over an obstruction. The Christian life is sometimes portrayed as a walk for this reason; the image of walking captures the idea of traveling, but with the greater likelihood of distraction than running a race. We can walk through our lives as if in a dream, listening to the opinions of the world around us, and miss everything that is important. When hardship strikes, it can focus our attention and bring us back to reality.

Life is fragile, and we need God's help. One of our first responses, when difficulties hit, should be, "You have my full attention, God! Your servant is listening" (see 1 Sam. 3:10). And as a second response, we should check to make sure our lives are on course. Tragedy offers us the chance to take stock of where we've come from and where we're headed. Not far ahead of all of us is a finish line. Everyone will cross it. The question is what kind of race we will have run when we do.

The vision of that moment must carry us when we are in pain and struggling. Our ability to gain strength and trust God through suffering is all about our perspective. We have to choose to forget what lies behind us and strain toward the goal, if we have the intent of arriving at all. The Lord provides us with the strength we need to do it, if we will trust and follow him. He is the one who helps us along the journey, present with us always, though unseen. But one day we *will* see him. He stands there, just beyond the finish line, with his arms open, waiting for us.

Chapter 2:
Purpose in Suffering

The world is covered in darkness. Nearly one and a half billion people live on less than $1.25 a day. Those who suffer the most don't get television coverage; they are largely invisible, as are the Christians who have dedicated themselves to bringing them hope and alleviating their suffering. Starving people don't make for compelling media content.

The UN estimates there are thirty million people globally who live as slaves, generating thirty-two billion dollars in revenue for human traffickers. Precise numbers are impossible to obtain because human trafficking is illegal and therefore hidden from direct examination. More so than any other crime, slavery is kept in darkness.

We are all struggling. We are managing stress, depression, and temptation. We're dealing with some measure of hidden sins, addictive habits, and self-destructive patterns. Some of us are burdened with medical problems. Others with financial concerns. We have fears and worries and do whatever we can to manage them. Some people suffer through abuse. Others of us are lonely and don't feel loved. We live in a world that has tragedy and brings pain and loss. The world is controlled by evil, and the effects of sin surround us and impact our lives. We are all surrounded by darkness. When we look at social problems and global suffering, all the way down to the troubles we each face every day, it seems like darkness is winning.

I have good news to share with you. It is a truth to hold onto when you find yourself losing hope: "The light shines in the darkness, and the darkness has not overcome it" (John 1:5).

When things seem darkest, you need to remember this. You need to embrace Jesus's statement that whoever follows him will not walk in darkness but will have the light of life (John 8:12). Jesus is the light of the world. The darkness around us does not mean he has lost or that his promises have been forgotten. It means only that darkness is permitted for a time. That is true of the world as a whole, and it is true of our lives.

The "Why" of Our Suffering

If God is all powerful, why would he permit sin and evil to exist? Why wouldn't he remove suffering, if he could? People have raised this question for thousands of years, and some use it as grounds for disbelief in God. When we experience pain and hardship, we demand answers from God. Why didn't you prevent this tragedy? Do you care about me? If the answers aren't clear to us, we may adopt our own solutions. One solution is that God is not loving. Another solution is that he is not real. Either way, we are left with the desperate and bitter sense that we are on our own.

There is nothing wrong with having questions. The Bible is filled with stories of men and women who struggled with hardship and wondered where God was in the middle of it. David asks this question in the opening to Psalm 22: "My God, my God, why have you forsaken me? Why are you so far from saving me, so far from my cries of anguish? My God, I cry out by day, but you do not answer, by night, but I find no rest" (Ps. 22:1-2). Gideon, who was one of the judges of Israel and a man of faith, directly questioned the angel of the Lord:

> *When the angel of the Lord appeared to Gideon, he said, "The Lord is with you, mighty warrior."*
>
> *"Pardon me, my lord," Gideon replied, "but if the Lord is with us, why has all this happened to us? Where are all his wonders that our ancestors told us about when they said, 'Did not the Lord*

> *bring us up out of Egypt?' But now the Lord has*
> *abandoned us and given us into the hand of Midi-*
> *an." (Judges 6:12-13)*

It's worth noting that Gideon doesn't get an explanation; what he receives instead is a working of God's
power in his own timing. We demand specific answers to our questions about pain and hardship and
assume we're owed an explanation. When one is not
forthcoming, we might invent our own. The atheist's
argument that God could not exist and also permit
evil and suffering is not much of an intellectual point;
there clearly can be a logical explanation, either with
respect to the timing of God's response or a lesson to
be learned through suffering, as was the case for Israel under Gideon's watch. It is, however, a compelling emotional point that is difficult to ignore. If we
don't feel that God is there for us, we may not trust
him. We might instead look for our own solutions
apart from his will.

I've demanded answers of God when I faced pain
and loss, just as Gideon did. I've doubted God's goodness at times in my life when things have not gone
well. I've wondered why God abandoned me, like David did, at times when I was desperate for his help.
All the while, he was there with me, loving me. Sus-
taining me through difficulty even when I chose not
to trust him. He never let me go. It has always taken
time and distance for me to recognize that. I haven't
always gotten answers, and I may never know the
specific reasons for some of the things I've gone
through. I have, however, experienced a working of

his power in his own timing. The question is if we will place our cares in his hands when new difficulties arise, knowing he has always proven faithful in the past. It's a challenge that confronts all of us. By understanding the bigger picture of our suffering, we can gain courage and trust his goodness. There *is* a bigger picture.

Suffering is Part of Our Destiny

Suffering is part of our destiny. It is not in contradiction to God's promises or proof that his plan has gone wrong. It may be tragic and difficult to understand, but we must expect hardship as followers of Christ. If we expect it, we are better equipped to handle it when it occurs. Hardship and pain is not a ripple on our sea of promised happiness but part of a process that leads to his transforming power. The suffering we endure in the present and the glory that awaits us are connected. We cannot demand the result without the steps needed to reach it. Paul, in fact, makes the end result conditional on the process: "Now if we are children, then we are heirs—heirs of God and co-heirs with Christ, if indeed we share in his sufferings in order that we may also share in his glory" (Rom. 8:17).

Jesus's suffering was not a sign the Father was not for him or that the Father didn't love him. His sufferings were directly related to the glory he achieved. There was purpose and meaning to what he went through. Following him through this dark world necessarily means difficulties for us as well. Jesus told his followers, "In this world you will have trouble. But take heart! I have overcome the world" (John 16:33). The trouble he refers to is the same trouble he faced himself; the victory he speaks of is also something we share. We achieve victory over pain and suffering the same way he did. That means, by being faithful and sticking to the path before us, no matter how difficult it may be. In the end, we will achieve eternal glory.

Despite the trouble we will face, Jesus tells us to take heart—there is victory over sin, pain, and suffering. Paul is encouraging us with this vision of the future, as well as challenging us to persevere in the present. If we share in Jesus's sufferings, we will also share in his destiny.

Our suffering has meaning and purpose for the same reason his did. The journey that led him to the cross is ours to share if we choose to follow him. Jesus makes it clear that anyone who would follow him must deny themselves and take up their cross (Mark 8:34-35). That was the road he walked. Along that road, we can expect difficulties as well. As his servants, we cannot demand an unbroken string of happy moments in this life. At least, not the level of comfort and entertainment that the world characterizes as essential for happiness. If you follow him in this life, you will share in his sufferings. But you will also share in his victory, power, and abundant life. In reflecting on it, Paul concludes, "I consider that our present sufferings are not worth comparing with the glory that will be revealed in us" (Rom. 8:18).

All of this leads to a change of perspective. Or at least, a shift in our expectations. We need to view our circumstances as part of a process that has, as its final goal, the same victory that Jesus accomplished over sin and death. Our suffering is connected to our destiny. Whatever life throws at you, it is nothing in comparison to what awaits you on the day you stand with the Lord.

Suffering is Part of Battle

Expecting some measure of pain and difficulty as we live for Christ doesn't explain why it is necessary or why Jesus's victory over sin and death doesn't extend to the problems we are facing. At least one thing is clear, though—the world as a whole has not changed as much as we might hope as a result of the cross. The hearts of countless individuals have been transformed by the Holy Spirit across the centuries, but the world is still in darkness.

In 1 John 5:19, we are reminded of two things we can know for certain: "We know that we are children of God, and that the whole world is under the control of the evil one." Knowing these things means accepting that we are going to meet resistance—that we have an identity that is inherently in conflict with the world around us. It explains why we cannot expect things to go smoothly all the time and why living out God's values will result in problems for us. At least part of the reason is that we have an enemy.

An exploration of Satan's purposes and strategy are beyond the scope of what I am writing here, but he is definitely in opposition to what Jesus Christ is doing in the world. That includes interfering with God's plan to bring salvation to the world, as well as undermining God's work in the lives of his children. Satan has significant resources to bring harm to us, and those resources are lodged in every culture, financial market, and political system on earth. They are directly under his control. Only the church itself stands in opposition to his power and agenda. Satan, and those who further his goals by submitting to his values, are the reason for the darkness that surrounds us.

If we live as children of the light, we will find ourselves in battle. We are caught up in a war between light and darkness. In Eph. 6, Paul writes: "Finally, be strong in the Lord and in his mighty power. Put on the full armor of God, so that you can take your stand against the devil's schemes" (Eph. 6:10-11). If we are in a battle, it follows that we can be harmed. There wouldn't be much sense in being told to put on our armor if we were invulnerable. Our battle, as Paul describes it, is both offensive and defensive. We have both a shield and a sword.

We engage not only the powers of this dark world but also the spiritual forces of evil in the heavenly realms. They are in league with one another. Our enemy is not flesh and blood, Paul tells us (Eph. 6:12), but the world our enemy controls *is* tangible. The world he refers to is the world we live in—the same one we see on television. The same one we work in to earn a living. He's not talking about the world in some intangible sense, but rather the actual world we occupy. If we regard Satan as a tempter but don't account for his involvement in the suffering and hardship we experience, we leave our flanks exposed. We have trivialized his participation as a byproduct of Western scientific thinking. He is actively engaged in bringing harm to God's children.

Labeling every bad thing that happens as Satan's doing is an oversimplification. There are many varied causes behind the pain we experience, and identifying all the direct and indirect influences behind our hardship or tragedy is likely to be impossible and a waste of time. What matters is our response. But any viewpoint on our lives that does not account for Satan's opposition is like riding into battle wearing nothing but our casual, everyday clothing. The full armor of God is necessary, Paul says, to take our stand against the devil's schemes. If we aren't wearing it, we will eventually get hurt.

When tragedy and loss strike us, we need to keep our defenses up. That is the point when we are the most vulnerable. It may, in fact, be the moment we enter the battleground Paul is referring to. Adopting a cultural solution to our pain, like venting our rage or drinking alcohol until we're numb, is a retreat. If we don't trust God actively and draw strength from him to stand up against Satan's lies, we can be drawn into even greater loss and despair. Satan wants nothing more than to drive as big a wedge between us and God as possible.

Faith, truth, and righteousness, as components of

the armor Paul describes, are not just ideas that keep us protected; they are behaviors. Temptation is a process that occurs in our minds but typically presents itself through physical objects and visual imagery. The pain, hardship, failure, tragedy, and evil that we experience are all part of Satan's control over the world. We experience these things as soldiers of the Most High God. We will continue to experience them until the world itself is remade (Rev. 21:1-5).

We can nonetheless have victory in battle as we wait for an end to the war. The victory we achieve is to stand firm and not be moved (Eph. 6:14). We cannot flee the world or entirely avoid physical types of evil, but we can resist temptation and remain steadfast in faith. We can respond to hardship by trusting God more than ever before and allowing him to bring us through it for his glory. This is the victory that we have over circumstances and hardship in our lives: not to allow these things to pull us off course when they strike.

Suffering is a Result of a Broken Creation

The world around us is *broken*. By that, I mean the world is in the grip of sin and death. It will one day be made new, which implies that the current state is not what God intended, though he clearly willed it to be so. The world is broken because he pronounced a curse. It was the consequence of sin (Gen. 3:17-19), but it was God's decision to respond to it this way. Does this mean the suffering that comes from calamities and natural disasters is his fault?

We see examples in the Bible of natural phenomena under God's control. The flood was a natural disaster that God used to bring judgment (Gen. 6:13). The fish that swallowed Jonah was sent by God both to transport the unwilling prophet and to give him three days in a troubling situation to teach him to embrace God's purposes (Jonah 1:17). These were unique incidents, though, and shouldn't be used to second-guess God's involvement in every tragic act of nature.

In asking why things have to be the way they are, we are really asking an even bigger question: *Was this necessary? Was there a way for humans to exercise free will, reject God's words, and then return to him through a process of trusting him that does not involve pain and suffering?* In his discussion on suffering in Rom. 8, Paul indicates that the world's condition is tied to our own redemption:

> *For the creation was subjected to frustration, not by its own choice, but by the will of the one who subjected it, in hope that the creation itself will be liberated from its bondage to decay and brought into the freedom and glory of the children of God. (Rom. 8:20-21)*

The phrase "in hope that" deserves our attention. The one who's hoping is *God*. He's the same one who subjected the creation to frustration in the previous clause. God's desire and hopeful anticipation is that we, his children, and the creation he gave us dominion over, would together experience freedom from the effects of sin. Our fates are tied together. The fact that he desires us to be liberated means he doesn't want it to be the way it is now.

The curse, despite its impact on our lives and the world around us, was the only way to get the final result. Jesus prayed, "Father, if you are willing, take this cup from me; yet not my will, but yours be done" (Luke 22:42). He's asking the Father to spare him the suffering ahead if it's not necessary. I think the prayer is spoken for our benefit, to help us understand the depth of his humanity and submission to the Father's will. Jesus knows that he would not have been sent to suffer if it were not necessary to save the world.

Contained within that prayer is the very thing God is hoping for, though, from us. He desires that his children would not repeat Adam's mistake but instead freely choose his will over their own, no matter what hardship lies before them. The end result will be the freedom and glory that Jesus provided for us. The fact that there may be suffering on that path is the thing that gives our decision meaning and significance.

The journey we take to reach our destiny passes through this broken world, with its suffering and tragedy. We must make the journey just as Jesus did, to reach the same destination as he did in the end. The process isn't pointless; we gain something by traveling the same way he did. Like Jesus, we must trust the Father. This broken world leaves us in a spot where we have the decision to do so in front of us, over and over. We not only have the need and reason to trust him, but he has the opportunity to reveal his faithfulness and power.

Suffering is a Result of Poor Choices

Many of the circumstances we deal with are the result of poor decisions we have made. They could be
direct consequences (such as crashing a car because
we are intoxicated) or indirect consequences (like
financial hardship as a result of bad investments). It
doesn't mean we are any less in need of help than
circumstances outside our control, but we have to
accept the fact that some of our suffering can be
traced back to choices we have made. The universe
has been constructed to operate by cause-and-effect.
This principle is sometimes known as *sowing and
reaping,* a phrase taken from Gal. 6:7-9. By God's
mercy, we may avoid some consequences of our poor
choices or be rescued from them, but more typically
we have to live in the aftermath.

One area where we suffer as a consequence of our
decisions is in the failure of relationships. We often
charge into a relationship despite clear indications it
is not in line with God's will for us. We also contrib-
ute to the failure of the relationship by our own sin.
When things fall apart, we are devastated and bitter
that God didn't rescue us, as if the decisions we made
leading up to that point were outside our control. In
the case of marriage, we may think that the ceremony
automatically guarantees God's blessing and protec-
tion against divorce, that the commitment we make
changes a bad decision into a good one. But this is a
misunderstanding of what marriage is and what a

ceremony accomplishes.

Like any decision, getting married to someone can be contrary to God's will, and therefore a sin. Scripture indicates at least two such conditions (Luke 16:18; 2 Cor. 6:14). The vows taken should be honored regardless, but the fact that they are made doesn't mean that God is in favor of the union or that we're not responsible for the consequences. If we seek his blessing, we obtain it by following him and pursuing righteousness. These are the only terms under which we can expect it. This may not be a comfort to those who have experienced a failed marriage, but it does bring an understanding of God's faithfulness in spite of it.

As we will see in chapter 5, God's love for us and desire to help us isn't conditional on whether or not we have brought problems on ourselves. As with all the reasons for our suffering, our responsibility for our troubles isn't as important as what we do in the middle of them. But they do help us recognize that there is at least this purpose in our suffering: that we learn to make wiser and godlier decisions in the future and stop repeating our failures. Prov. 26:11 puts this in colorful terms: "As a dog returns to its vomit, so fools repeat their folly." If we trust God, we obey him. The Bible knows no other understanding of faith. Hardship is one of the things that can break us from self-destructive patterns and lead us to the life he wants for us.

If we do trust God, then our suffering has more than just taught us to avoid sin. It has shown us how to choose life. If we sow to please the Spirit, as Paul says in Gal. 6:7-9, we end up not only avoiding destruction but gaining something: the life we have always wanted. It is eternal, in the sense that it never ends, but it begins now, not after we die. It is a powerful and transformed life, characterized by joy and peace. The way we achieve that life is by trusting Jesus Christ and following him. That trust happens in the context of the sin, pain, and difficulties in our lives.

Chapter 3:
The Case for Weakness

One of the reasons people play video games is because it makes them feel powerful and in control. In a virtual world, you get to be powerful (at least, you have the potential to *become* powerful, with time and practice). Games are becoming more like reality, and as they do, they change the way we think of ourselves. We all want to feel powerful. Being powerful is fun. Being weak and having life beat down on you is not fun.

The problem is that we don't live in a game. Our funds are limited, our bodily strength is less than superhuman, our physical appearance a little short of model-quality. We often find ourselves disappointed, with life taking a brutal toll on us. Sometimes other people bring disaster and pain into our lives, and, no matter how hard we try, we can't do anything about it. We feel underpowered, so we try to compensate by focusing on our strengths. We try to take control. We might even try to control others as a way to feel better about our own lives.

As a Christian, you can become bitter at God for allowing bad things to happen to you. I have done that. I spent years pleading with him to take some things away that were hurting me deeply. As time went on and those things didn't get removed, I made the decision to trust him regardless. Then something happened. I began to change.

The idea that our suffering can lead to a positive outcome is something we are all familiar with. Athletes have to experience some degree of pain as part of their training. An even better example is childbirth. I am sure many women have felt, at the point they were in labor, that God could have helped them more! Childbirth is a good analogy for the suffering in our lives because it is so clearly linked to the life it produces. You cannot obtain the result without suffering, and there is no more precious or worthwhile result. Paul uses this analogy in his discussion on suffering in Rom. 8:

> *We know that the whole creation has been groaning as in the pains of childbirth right up to the present time. Not only so, but we ourselves, who*

have the firstfruits of the Spirit, groan inwardly as we wait eagerly for our adoption to sonship, the redemption of our bodies. (Rom. 8:22-23)

In childbirth, the pain has a purpose. The suffering is temporary; it ends when the result is achieved. The pain gives even greater meaning to the life that comes after. It was born at a cost. The universe we live in reflects the same purposes. There is evil and suffering, but they are temporary. They are part of a process that will one day result in a new creation. The supposed contradiction between pain and suffering and God's love is removed when we understand that it is a necessary and transitional step in his plan to bring us something so much more significant.

The same is also true of our lives. Paul says in v. 23 that we groan as in the pains of childbirth as we wait for the redemption of our bodies. Like the creation, we too are in a process that will result in new life. The suffering we endure gives meaning to our faith as we trust him. It directs our attention to the day when all of this will be behind us, and we stand with our Savior in glory.

Understanding the purpose in suffering allows us to endure it, just like the examples mentioned. If we understand the purposes behind it, we are already prepared when things get difficult. The moment we are pulled toward a solution under our own power we can resist, receive God's strength, and wait for him to reveal himself.

Suffering Leads to God's Power

As mentioned earlier, Paul had some problem that tormented him, and we're not sure what it was. He calls it a *thorn in his flesh* in 2 Cor. 12:7, so it was apparently something in his body. We use this as a metaphor nowadays, but Paul's writing is the origin of the expression. It's most likely a health problem, given the language he uses. Whatever it was, though, there are a few things we are sure of. We are sure that it caused him serious pain. We are sure that it was sent by Satan and was intended to harm him. And we are certain that God not only refused to remove it but that he used it to change Paul's life.

> *Therefore, in order to keep me from becoming conceited, I was given a thorn in my flesh, a messenger of Satan, to torment me. Three times I pleaded with the Lord to take it away from me. But he said to me, "My grace is sufficient for you, for my power is made perfect in weakness." Therefore I will boast all the more gladly about my weaknesses, so that Christ's power may rest on me. That is why, for Christ's sake, I delight in weaknesses, in insults, in hardships, in persecutions, in difficulties. For when I am weak, then I am strong. (2 Cor. 12:7-10)*

This passage gives critical insights into suffering. First, it tells us that the evil one can bring horrible things into our lives; we are not immune to that, as Christians. It teaches us that, when we face pain and hardship, it is not necessarily the case that we have done anything wrong. It also shows that we cannot always see God's specific purposes in allowing hardship to come on us. But his general purpose is clear: He wants us to become weak.

This is not something that we want to hear, but it is true. As we fight for power and control over the circumstances in our lives, we lose the opportunity to rest in the hands of our Savior. Our strengths, our triumphs, our wealth, our physical beauty—we can choose to lean on these things, or we can lean on the one who is Lord over all. If we do find ourselves beaten down, hurt, in desperate straits, or the victim of someone's anger or betrayal, we are also in the perfect position to experience his power. God's power is perfected in our weakness.

If our wills and personal resources are strong enough, more difficulty may result in more room for him to work. This was apparently the case with Paul. Our conceit and self-will interfere with experiencing his transforming power. We must decrease for him to increase. Our humility, loss, and pain are the perfect condition for him to do something incredible in and through us. As difficult as that may be to accept in the middle of our suffering, we need to recognize that we are on the verge of seeing God do something amazing in our lives. If we think that way, we can experience true freedom and find ourselves closer to becoming the people we were meant to be.

Paul doesn't describe what we need to do to experience God's power, because it should be evident that suffering, by itself, doesn't necessarily have this result. It's dependent on us. But Paul was able to achieve it through hardship. And in his repeated difficulty, an even greater result was achieved. This isn't exactly the most encouraging news for those of us going through hard times, but it does put each of us at the crossroads of decision. *Do I want to experience God's power? Will I trust him when I experience pain, loss, and hardship?*

The choice we are making is the choice to become the people we are meant to be and experience the blessings he wants for us, or to stay where we're at. Generally speaking, we experience anxiety, despair, and emptiness. We want more from life but don't know how to get it. We follow the path our culture dictates, trying to earn more money and acquire more possessions, and find ourselves more miserable than ever. We have bought into the lie that we will be happier if we avoid suffering and achieve the Hollywood version of the good life. And all along, the solution is staring us in the face. Life—the true life that God offers to all of us—comes only by trusting him, and that trust occurs in a life filled with disappointment and pain. We achieve everything we really want and need in a manner that is the opposite of what Hollywood tells us. We become fulfilled when we walk through suffering with our eyes firmly locked on the one who waits before us with his arms outstretched. We not only follow the same path he did, but we experience the same joy.

I've had men tell me they don't feel close to God and are not experiencing his joy. It's a recurring problem in our culture, particularly with men. We've bought into a cultural definition of what it means to be a man—that it's about being strong and taking control of your life. But the key to becoming who we are meant to be, whether male or female, is to submit to God and let him meet us in our weakness. We need to grab hold of him and walk with him through the ups and downs of life. We need to find our way to his plan and abandon our own. Down that path is an experience of his presence, joy, and transforming power.

Paul says he delights in his weaknesses. Some years back, something terrible happened to me that I could not control and did not deserve, and, for the first time ever, I felt joy, knowing that God would reveal himself even more powerfully in my life. I have never had what people call a "life verse," but it struck me that 2 Cor. 12:9 was that, for me. My perspective changed on hardship—on all the things I think are so good about me and all the things I think are so bad. I need to rejoice in all the things that make me weak and dependent on Christ. God has changed me through the hardships I faced because I trusted him. I wouldn't have it any other way, from where I stand now.

If you take a stand for Christ and pursue the life that God wants for you, things will not always go well. You will have pain, discouragement, hardship, and loss. You will also have a chance to see incredible things happen through your life. It is not the reason why bad things happen, but it is the purpose.

The Explanation of Weakness

We live in a world of the rich and powerful. We watch the lives of celebrities unfold with the same drama as the movies they star in. They crash and burn in a seemingly never-ending cycle of marriage, divorce, addiction, and rehab, but somehow still hold onto millions of fans. Some people achieve high levels of wealth with lifestyles the rest of us can only dream about. Still others achieve political power that allows them to wield legislative influence and military might and set policies that are life and death for those under their control. They are all variations of worldly power—fame, fortune, and force. God wants nothing to do with them.

When Jesus begins his ministry, we see exhibitions of power but nothing like the kind of power that people normally wield. He calms the storm and walks on water to show he is the Creator of heaven and earth. He removes disease and brings people back from the dead to prove he is the giver of life. These are not displays of power for their own sake but to confirm his identity and reveal his love. Even in those cases, it was rare that more than a few people stood witness to his power. An exception is the feeding of the five thousand, and, in that case, the story takes an interesting turn. Jesus has the disciples take him across the Sea of Galilee after he dismisses the crowds (Matt 14:22). At the moment he was best able to distill strength from numbers, he intentionally causes the crowd to disperse. Sheer numbers were a sign of worldly power. Jesus wanted none of it.

What we need to accept is that God intentionally works in ways that bring him glory and expose efforts apart from him as futile. The way he does that is by working through weakness. If a strong man lifts a heavy weight, it's clear that he's doing it because he's strong. But if a weak man lifts the same weight, it's equally obvious that he's getting some help. The attention turns from the man to the bigger question: *What is the force that brings this help?* And to the further question: *Why is help being offered?* The answer to these questions is only pressing because the man is weak. We don't ask out of idle curiosity but because we want the same help when we need to lift something beyond our own strength. If you can track through the example, you know everything you need to know to understand why our weakness is the opportunity for his power.

In 1 Corinthians, Paul is writing to a church split by factions. There were different opinions about matters of worship and purity. Groups were polarizing behind several leaders, of which Paul was one. One of the criticisms leveled at Paul, we can infer, is that he wasn't a compelling speaker. Paul's response is in his own defense, but it happens to give us insight into the way God works: "But God chose the foolish things of the world to shame the wise; God chose the weak things of the world to shame the strong. God chose the lowly things of this world and the despised things—and the things that are not—to nullify the things that are, so that no one may boast before him"

(1 Cor. 1:27-29).

If God works powerfully through someone who wields worldly power, no questions are asked. The assumption is that the person did as expected. But when God works through someone who is weak in the world's eyes, all attention turns to God. Not only to bring glory to God but to inquire about his purposes. *What kind of a God works through broken and humble people? Why would he?* When you find out the answer, you have in your hands the most wonderful news imaginable. He does it because he loves us and wants us to trust him. It's great news because we all need that love. Our weakness is the way God communicates his love for the world and his desire to work through every human life.

We spend our lives trying to figure out how to be as strong as possible. We strive for success, motivated by our ambition to stand on our own. And all the way, God was ready to meet us at the point we were the most broken and needy. Even the powerful need him, but they don't know it. It's for this reason that Jesus's ministry was so often focused on the outcasts of society or on the ritually unclean. Very few from the upper echelons of his culture found their way to him, but not because he wasn't willing to offer them the same life he did others. They didn't listen because they didn't think they needed what he was selling. Worldly success can have the effect, blinding us to our true need. Sometimes the only way the powerful and mighty accept their neediness is by a hardship they can't control.

What we learn from this is that, to the degree our triumphs, skills, and ambition substitute for reliance on God, they are an impediment. They block us from the life we truly need. Even when things are going well, we need to see ourselves as men and women who can't do it apart from the one who created us. We must walk in humility as his servants. If the only way to bring us to that spot is tragedy, then he might use it to help us accept our weakness. If so, it's just a reminder of the humility we should recognize and practice every day. If we embrace our weakness and rest in his strength, we can make it through every season of life without wavering.

The Result of Weakness

One of the big lessons in life is accepting your limits. I was in the gym awhile back, trying to lift too much weight, forgetting for a moment that I was no longer twenty-five. It was a very brief moment, I can tell you. I could feel a tendon pop in my hamstring as I released the dumbbell. I knew I was going to have to lower my expectations for myself if I really was shooting to be here for the long haul.

When we are young, we feel invincible. It's a shame we don't get an opportunity to experience life at fifty-something while we're young; it would change our perspective. We'd be more likely to understand that we're not as strong as we think we are, that we can't charge through life and remain unscathed. We have limits, and we will eventually reach them. There is no benefit in thinking less of yourself than you really are. We need to take risks and set our sights on doing great things. But knowing we are weak can lead us to a source of power that is greater than the challenges and discouragements we face along the way.

Paul was someone who failed. He was a man who persecuted the Lord he later served. He was aware of his weaknesses and difficulties and reveled in them because they provided an opportunity for God's power. So much so that he depicts himself and his coworkers as jars of clay—lowly and fragile vessels which contain God's glory:

> But we have this treasure in jars of clay to show that this all-surpassing power is from God and not from us. We are hard pressed on every side, but not crushed; perplexed, but not in despair; persecuted, but not abandoned; struck down, but not destroyed. We always carry around in our body the death of Jesus, so that the life of Jesus may also be revealed in our body. For we who are alive are always being given over to death for Jesus's sake, so that his life may also be revealed in our mortal body. So then, death is at work in us, but life is at work in you. (2 Cor. 4:7-12)

Paul analogy is more than a word picture; it describes the condition under which God's power appears. God's power happens in our lives when our limitations are revealed. Those limitations are never more apparent than when we suffer. If in the moments we face pain, loss, and hardship we turn to Christ, we provide him the opportunity to draw attention to himself. In that moment of clarity, others will see and desire the powerful, transforming life that Jesus offers. Our weakness is a component in God's plan of salvation for the world. It's how Jesus draws people to himself.

It's a paradox. One would expect that our strength would attract people to the Lord, but it is the opposite. Having perfect, seamless lives that blend together with the best this world has to offer provides little opportunity for the Lord. Having beauty, affluence, and incredible natural abilities can create plausible denial. It permits another explanation for the positive elements in our lives than Jesus Christ. It can draw people toward us instead of to him. It can disconnect us from those who don't have it all together and need a solution to their pain and sin.

What people are looking for is someone as broken and empty as they are but who has found hope and new life. This is what Jesus offers to those who walk in darkness—the light of life (John 8:12). The more clearly that light shines, the easier for them to find their way to it. It is never more visible than in the lives of those who suffer but have trusted him.

Paul's words in 2 Corinthians, cited above, are difficult to unravel, but he points the way to the reasons why Christ has worked so powerfully in and through his life. He says that he always carries the death of Jesus in his body so that the life of Jesus would be revealed. The *death of Jesus* is his participation in Jesus's sufferings, as described earlier (Phil. 3:10; Rom. 8:17). It includes the things he lists—being hard pressed, perplexed, persecuted, and struck down. These were the result of living out Jesus's values. The *life of Jesus* is the transforming power that is at the center of his ministry.

That power is not just something for eternity; Paul lets us know that this power is "revealed in our mortal body" (2 Cor. 4:11). It is for the here-and-now. We know it is to bring others to salvation because, as he says, "death is at work in us, but life is at work in you" (v. 12). In other words, the outworking of this power led to the salvation of the very people he is writing to.

The life of Jesus in our mortal bodies that Paul mentions is just what it sounds like. It is Jesus's life *in us*. He took our place on the cross, and we receive his life. That life is everything you would expect it to be. It is powerful enough to carry you through this life and into the next one. It has meaning and purpose. The purpose it has is Jesus's purpose—we receive his life, and along with that, we receive his mission. Our lives have incredible meaning if we live that purpose out. We find ourselves drawn into God's plan for the world. We are used by him as ministers of his love. If we turn away from our own selfish plans and seek his, we will also find we are accompanied by his power. It is real, miraculous, and relevant. It leads us into situations where we can accomplish his goals. It's not for those who pursue their own agenda.

In our suffering, we are identifying with the Lord, and, in doing so, we find ourselves at the center of God's will, on the same path Jesus walked. Everyone is on course to the end of their physical lives, but we have our sights set beyond it. We need to finish this part of the journey by trusting the Father no matter what life throws at us, knowing that the difficulty is what we should expect. But we should also expect to see him do amazing things within us, and through us, to others.

Some of the hardships I have faced over the years have been outside my control, and others I am directly responsible for. I can be hard on myself, and it's been difficult not to spend time in regret. But I have hope. God chose the foolish and weak things of the world so that the true source of wisdom and power would become evident, and no one could boast (1 Cor. 1:27-28). I know that in writing those words, Paul counts himself as one of those foolish and weak things. I am one of them also.

The suffering I have experienced has forced me to trust God and accept my weaknesses. My desire is for God to reveal himself through the person I am now. I don't believe I could have reached this point or written these words if I hadn't traveled along this path. My prayer is for you also, that his transforming power would help you become all you are meant to be as you trust him through difficult times.

Chapter 4:
Pride and Consequences

Self-sufficiency is a value in our culture today. Getting by without the help of others is one of the goals of life. If you manage to pull it off, you feel capable and in control of your life. Our self-worth in today's world is our ability to provide for ourselves and others. With the loss of a job or some financial hardship, you can spiral down and feel like your life has little meaning. Nothing feels more humiliating than being incapable of providing for yourself.

Not long ago, at a point when unemployment was peaking, I rode in an Uber car with a young man who had completed his master's degree in mechanical engineering. He had been trying for a year to find an entry-level position as an engineer but had repeatedly struck out. He was getting by as a driver, but I could hear discouragement in his voice as he shared his struggles with me. Circumstances had trapped him in a downward spiral of self-worth. I told him things wouldn't always be this difficult, but until he saw himself differently, whether he was on top of the world or tumbling downhill, he wouldn't experience the joy he was meant to have. He would be a prisoner to the extremes of pride and despair, controlled by circumstances never fully under his control.

When things go well, we can feel capable and powerful. We invest our lives in our own security, working hard to keep everything running smoothly. The desire to prevent financial hardship can drive us to extremes, both in the way we view ourselves and the way we see God. It can take over and control our lives and substitute the world's values for God's. It can put us at odds with others or on a solitary climb to success. We were not meant to be completely self-reliant; we were created to trust God. We were intended to serve him first and pursue our individual self-interests second. If we confuse our obligation to work hard and provide for our families with the vision of self-sufficiency and independence our culture idealizes, we won't become the people we were meant to be or have the life we were meant to have.

Pride, more than anything in today's world, has the capability of robbing us of the life Jesus offers. It can neutralize us and keep us focused on ourselves while the years tick by. It can cause us to spend all our waking moments in pursuits that are empty and shallow. It can decimate the relationships we need the most and isolate us from true love. If we fall into the pride-delusion, disaster in our lives may be the only thing that grabs our attention and causes us to focus on what really matters.

As an act of mercy, God sometimes intervenes and allows things in our lives to fall apart to save us from ourselves. It was certainly the case with me. Understanding how pride traps you can help you when things do go badly. Identifying your self-centeredness can help you find your way to God's purposes and turn disaster into a blessing. Rejecting pride and escaping its lure is a critical step in finding your way to the abundant life Christ offers you.

The Most Prideful Man Who Ever Lived

Our culture today tells us to focus on ourselves as a way to keep us locked into a cycle of work and consumption. The system needs us to be selfish individualists to keep selling superficial products and services. The moment we realize the car we drive doesn't say anything important about us as human beings is the death of a large segment of the automobile industry. But we're in no danger of that; we've long-since accommodated ourselves to the sense that the job we have, our possessions, and our ability to enjoy ourselves are the ways we reveal our true selves to the world and obtain the keys to the life we want.

We want what we want, and we want it now because *it's all about us*, we think. Pride makes the modern world we live in possible.

Roughly six centuries before the birth of Christ, a pagan emperor by the name of Nebuchadnezzar wrote about his struggle with pride in Daniel 4. It's the only chapter in the Bible written by a pagan, though it reflects a work of God in his life that Christians need to pay attention to because the attitude we see in his life is typical of the world today. Nebuchadnezzar had good reason to think highly of himself; he could enact any law he chose, sentence any of his subjects to death, and enjoy any pleasure imaginable. His wealth was essentially endless, his judgment unquestioned. He found his value and worth in his power. He believed he needed nothing and no one. That misunderstanding prevented him from knowing who he was and reaching the life he was meant to have. God, in his mercy, didn't let him continue under that delusion.

It's All About Me

God reaches Nebuchadnezzar in a dream. God has a very important message for him, and there is no one brave enough to deliver it to Nebuchadnezzar. God has to do it. Even if someone else told Nebuchadnezzar, he wouldn't choose to believe them. Pride protects us from hearing the truth. It's a defense mechanism. It's a way to harden yourself and justify what you want. People who think it's *all about them* don't listen to advice.

We become deaf when we focus on ourselves and ignore what matters, when we spend all our energy getting what we want. We think we have it figured out. Like I mentioned earlier, I think it might be worse for men than women because we're told that being strong, self-sufficient, and self-determined is what it means to be a man. Being humble, relying on other people, serving others, and subordinating yourself to a higher will are not the characteristics the world associates with manliness. We're not taught to listen; we're taught to tell others what to do. That's what a leader is, in our culture. Have any of you men ever been told you're a bad listener? I have.

You won't listen to people if you think you have it all figured out. You won't take advice if you don't think you make mistakes or don't want to admit it. That's pride, and we're set up for it. The world around us teaches us to think that way and makes it possible to live as if it were true. We believe we are at the center of everything and we've lost the ability to see anything else. You can see how someone might go too far and cross a moral line if they were in a position of power, like so many high-profile figures in government and the media. You know they had wakeup calls, people telling them to back off, but they couldn't hear. It was all about them—what *they* wanted. We fall into the same trap.

God tries to speak to us—other people try, too—but we're hardened because we're in pursuit of what we want. You can't find your way to the life God has for you if you won't listen. You *can* find your way to a disaster that ruins your life, though. Humility isn't weakness; it's wisdom. A wise person puts themselves in a spot where others feel comfortable challenging their decisions. Wise people don't argue just because someone disagrees with them. These are symptoms of our pride. They are signs we are not who we should be and that we don't have the life God wants for us.

Daniel comes before Nebuchadnezzar, who recounts his dream (Dan. 4:13-17). It's not just a dream, it's a nightmare—a vision of a great tree that is chopped down, leaving only a stump. It depicts a man standing in the rain with the mind of an animal. An angel decrees these things will come to pass so that everyone might know that God is sovereign over *all* rulers. When Nebuchadnezzar finishes, Daniel stands silent. He knew what the dream meant. But it was a dream about judgment, and Daniel is afraid to tell Nebuchadnezzar. He's probably scared of what the king will do to the messenger who delivers the bad news.

This is another sign of pride, by the way: people are afraid to talk to you. They don't want to tell you you're making a mistake because they're worried about your reaction. But fortunately, Nebuchadnezzar trusts Daniel. So he tells him not to be alarmed but to speak his mind (v. 19).

Daniel apologizes for being the bearer of bad news, but God was going to bring judgment on Nebuchadnezzar, he says, taking away his kingdom and his sanity for seven years. But Nebuchadnezzar will be restored afterward, which is why the stump remains in the dream. But not until he looks up and acknowledges that God is sovereign above all kingdoms, including his own. In other words, Nebuchadnezzar, you will live with consequences until you admit *it's not all about you*. You can't do whatever you want, as if there were no consequences and no higher authority.

Whatever I Want

We want to do whatever we want. In fact, this is the thing we shoot for. No bosses, no limitations. That's freedom, in our culture. When we tell someone, *Don't tell me what to do*, our response sounds like an expression of a fundamental right or an ideal. We believe we're standing up for ourselves. But these are the words of pride. They really mean: *I know what's best*. They are defensive words that keep us from having to change.

Pride is like a prison. It locks you in your sin. It separates you from blessings. It prevents you from growing. It keeps you from the life you were meant to have in Christ. You don't get that life by doing whatever you want. You get it from humility. Humility is the opposite of what culture tells us is the best kind of life.

One of the reasons Christianity doesn't appeal to young people in Western culture is because doing whatever you want is an ideal. Christianity seems to take our freedom away and ruin our fun.

Humility is freedom from our sin. Saying, *I choose*

to do what you want, Lord, is not losing freedom, it's gaining. You gain fulfillment as you accept the life you were created for. The life you were created for is a life of holiness. It's not enough to *listen* to advice, to receive that kind of life; you need to *take* advice. You need to stop justifying what you're doing wrong if you want to feel close to God and see him work in your life. Your pride is hurting you.

God gives Nebuchadnezzar a year to change. One year to listen to what Daniel said. Do you think he will listen? Do you think he will change and become humble?

> *Twelve months later, as the king was walking on the roof of the royal palace of Babylon, he said, "Is not this the great Babylon I have built as the royal residence, by my mighty power and for the glory of my majesty?" (Dan. 4:29-30)*

Guess what? No change. It's still all about him. Pride often doesn't change. If you won't listen, if you're blind to your sin, you might never change. Sometimes the only thing that can stop us is for everything to fall apart.

If your selfish plans fail, if you're caught in your sin and exposed, if your finances crash, your marriage crumbles, you lose your job and all the things you trust in, all the things you think you're in control of, and all the things you use to make yourself happy—you have a chance to stop and look up. Because sometimes disaster is the only thing that can save us from something even bigger: wasting our lives in self-deception, destroying ourselves and those closest to us as we put ourselves first and make everything about us. Hardship in your life can be a gift, or, at least, a chance to get on track and have the life you're supposed to have.

I went through a phase in my life when I thought I had it all worked out. I didn't need anyone. I had my life under control. I was blind to my sin, and I wasn't open with anyone about it. I was doing whatever I wanted. Everything was going great. Then all the sudden, it wasn't. Everything I thought I had control of fell apart. Looking back on it, it was God's grace or else I wouldn't be writing these words. I'd be wasting my life on things that don't matter at all. I would have reached the end and had nothing to show for my time here. But he loved me too much to let me do that.

God loves us all more than that. So what that means is that, by his grace, for our own good, God may break our pride.

We were created to be servants of the Lord. His children. We can't receive his blessings, know him, and have the life he wants for us if we have pride. If we think it's all about us, if we're blind to our sin, doing whatever we want, we can't have the life God created us to have. If we're lucky, though, he will stop us from wasting our lives by getting our attention.

Those media icons and public figures caught in sexual exploitation were stopped. I don't know if they understand that it was for their own good or not. I doubt they're looking at it that way, but they should. I don't know if they will look up and acknowledge God and put him at the center and not themselves. But Nebuchadnezzar did. If you do, you are saved from yourself. You can know the Lord, and find your way to the life he has for you. To that moment when you can say, *It's all about you, Lord.* All the blessings he wants for his children follow from those words.

Our Sanity Restored

The events in the dream came true. Nebuchadnezzar had seven years of insanity, losing everything, but he was saved. He gained something. He came to know who God was, and in comparison, who he was. "At the end of that time, I, Nebuchadnezzar, raised my eyes toward heaven, and my sanity was restored. Then I praised the Most High" (Dan. 4:34).

As horrible as the corruption is that we see among the powerful and elite of our time, Jesus has new life for them, too—if they will look up. He has the same for you if you're caught in pride. This pagan man, this despot, Nebuchadnezzar—if God can save him from his pride, he can save anyone. And he apparently does save Nebuchadnezzar. When his sanity is restored, he finds the words he needed all along: "Now I, Nebuchadnezzar, praise and exalt and glorify the King of heaven, because everything he does is right and all his ways are just. And those who walk in pride he is able to humble" (Dan. 4:36-37).

His acknowledgment is the key—it's how we find our way from tragedy and disaster to the life we need. We will discuss the idea further in the next chapter.

God humbles us as an expression of his grace and love. Our dreams, our selfish plans, the things we pursue out of arrogance—those can all come to an end. But God's plans for you, if you will trust him, can't be stopped. The world tells you that if you don't take care of yourself and get all you can while you're able, you're missing out. *It's all about you, so do whatever you want.* But when children trust their loving Father, he takes care of them. They experience his joy and provision. You don't lose anything if you humble yourself and live as a child of God; you gain. The disasters we see in the media are not happening in spite of our cultural values; they're happening because of them. Those who fell did what the world told them, not what the Lord wants for all of us.

God wants us all to know that our sense of control and self-sufficiency is insanity that prevents us from real joy and fulfillment. Pride holds us captive in the middle of the circumstances of our lives, either good or bad. It keeps us from changing and becoming what we are supposed to be. If we believe we have control over life, we are just one step from the ground giving way beneath us. Sometimes the way to see that is to stumble and recognize we're not as capable as we think, to escape an even greater disaster we can't find our way out of. When we reach hardship, we have the opportunity to look at our attitude and priorities and make a correction before it's too late.

Freedom, Blessing, and Love

God wants us to know that our pride stands in the

way of his blessing. We were created to be reliant on him, like a child is to their parent. In our culture this sounds like failure, but only because we've looked at things incorrectly from the beginning. We value a life of self-dependency because the world lives like God doesn't exist. It teaches us values that don't make sense of our purpose. If we were created in his image and intended to come into a loving relationship with him, then relying on him is the key to our existence. We find love, identity, and eternal life when we see ourselves as dependent on our Father in heaven. Rebelling against him and claiming we can do it on our own is a recipe for disaster, the same way it would be for any children of loving parents.

The loving parent provides for their children. The relationship brings freedom, not limitation. Having a place in a loving family means we don't do it on our own, and we don't have to. If we try to, we're keeping ourselves from the very relationship that helps us reach our potential.

God uses hardship to lead us to the truth, to reorient us and put us on the path we were made for. We don't want to accept that he might be the reason behind the difficulties we face, but we share the same motivation as he does when our children are making self-destructive decisions. Our love for them is too great to let them hurt themselves if we have the means to stop them. Withholding financial assistance from a child who is a drug addict might not feel like love, but when their car is repossessed, it might give them a chance to think about the decisions they are making. The child might not experience it that way, but that's just emotion. Love isn't emotion; it's an act on behalf of another, to offer them the thing they need, not necessarily what they want.

Understood in this sense, our difficulties can be an expression of God's love. They can help us choose life and avoid death. We often enable the self-destructive tendencies of our children; we think that giving them what they want is an expression of love, and we dislike the experience of rejection when we deny them their requests. But God is too wise to be drawn to that fallacy and too good to give us something that isn't ideal for us.

If we think the strategy holds true for our kids but not for our own lives, we're deceiving ourselves. I have one life—one chance to get things right. If I am going to ruin it out of stubbornness, foolishness, or delusion, then the catastrophe that God allows or even brings on my life is an act of mercy. In the end, I am going to stand with him. Despite the pain that hardship causes me today, I don't want to be ashamed when that day comes.

Jesus asked a critical question in Mark 8:36. We need to stop and think about it the next time we're feeling bitter over some discipline God brings to our lives. He asked, "What good is it for someone to gain the whole world, yet forfeit their soul?" (Mark 8:36). It's a rhetorical question; nothing is worth losing your eternal soul over. If losing wealth, a relationship or material possessions will save our souls, then good riddance to them. It's better to lose the world than eternity with God.

If we can accept that, we can find in the mystery of our suffering the strength to trust God's love and seek his face. I have been in that spot many times, convinced that I had things right, pleading for God to change my circumstances. But I was off course, wasting my time and energy on things that didn't matter. His discipline was for my good. We must remember that "the Lord disciplines the one he loves, and he chastens everyone he accepts as his son" (Heb. 12:6). He loved me too much to give me what I wanted.

Chapter 5:
Sovereign Over All

Life is like a jigsaw puzzle. Our experiences give rise to questions we need to solve. We can feel discouraged as we stand over a pile of pieces that don't fit together the way we've been told. Our failed dreams, the mistakes we keep repeating, the hardships that overtake us, and the challenges that lie before us—they can overwhelm and confuse us in a world that tells us to find happiness at any cost. Like any puzzle, the pieces only make sense if we have the right solution. They form a picture of God's power and love that can lead us to the joy and fulfillment we're all looking for. The world offers no guidance to reach the life we need. It makes no sense of our struggles and offers no permanent solution to our pain. But Christianity does. If we approach life with the right picture in mind, we have a much easier time solving the puzzle of what life is all about and why things go wrong.

In our culture, God is often thought of as distant and uncaring. It's a convenient excuse to speed along on our own journey and ignore the idea that he wants us to live a certain way. We focus our lives on things that meet our needs more quickly than he does. We focus on pursuits that we consider important, centered on our personal vision of happiness. These things leave us distracted and disconnected from any sense that God is near and paying attention to us.

When difficulties catch up with us and God is nowhere to be found, we forget we abandoned him a few onramps back on the superhighway of our lives, and his apparent absence is really what we should expect if we don't treat him as being important. These are all misconceptions of God, though, and the best way we can derive meaning from our suffering is to know him more deeply before difficulties overtake us. His power and love are the big picture we require to assemble the broken pieces of our lives.

We're not always going to understand the reason for difficulties, and it's precisely for this reason that the Christian life is a matter of trust. Our understanding is limited, and the reasons behind the circumstances of life aren't something that can always be expressed in simple terms. Tragedy today can mean blessings many years in the future; there is no way for us to see the final picture without following a path through heartache to reach the final outcome. The question is not the reason why it's happening but whether we will trust him. Doing so requires that we know him as he is. You can't trust someone you don't really know.

We begin this chapter by reflecting on some individuals who learned about God's sovereignty in the middle of difficulties. As we review the lessons they learned, we can gain a higher perspective on our own lives.

Understanding Who God Is and Who We Are

Our culture is focused on the individual. We think we know what's best and we're worried that doing what God wants may result in a worse version of life than what we'd pick for ourselves. It's especially difficult to trust God in our day and age because the world around us offers us so many ways to get our needs met as individuals. It promises a solitary kind of happiness, if only we have enough money and freedom to make our dreams come true. We treasure our freedom, which we think of as being able to choose whatever we want. We even envision this idea that God wants us to be happy and to pursue our own dreams. It's not a surprise that, when things don't work out, we start to question God.

When I think of a biblical character who doesn't know God very well, I think of Jonah. Jonah found himself in pursuit of his own preferences. He was a prophet, ordered to preach a message of repentance to the Ninevites, but he decided to ignore God and do what he thought was best. His vision of happiness was to get as far from Ninevah as possible. His response is understandable; the Ninevites were a bloodthirsty and vicious people, and it was unlikely they'd respond well to a message of judgment for their sin. Jonah may have reasoned that his best interests were served by a detour...to the other side of the known world. He probably thought he was saving himself. But this was a misconception. The God who commanded him was more powerful than the circumstances of life. His order wasn't one option among many; it was the will of the King of Heaven and Earth. You can't run far enough to get away him.

We can't fault Jonah, though; we're all a little like him. We pursue our dreams, unsure of God's faithfulness and ability to help us. Treating his plan like it is one option among many to have a happy life is something we've been taught by the world around us, which values all religious opinions as equally valid. We often run from the thing we are meant to do and the kind of people we should be in favor of an image the world portrays. We let Hollywood tell us how to be happy, and we believe no one is more qualified to get us there than ourselves.

We live in a culture of self, where we not only think we know best but that getting what we want is the goal of our lives. It's a kind of idolatry but not the little statues of gods from Jonah's time. We place ourselves at the center and we act like everything is *for* us and *about* us. Idolatry is the practice of focusing our devotion and priorities on something other than God. If we don't focus on him, the next likeliest candidate for our devotion is ourselves. In doing that, we misunderstand who God is. He's not one option among many; he's the Lord above all things. We are beneath him. He deserves our attention, devotion, and obedience. When we offer it to him, we fulfill the purpose for which we were created. It's not subservience in some negative sense; it's the kind of relationship we were made to experience. Living like we're the center of the universe blocks that plan. It keeps us from our potential and all that goes with it.

Riding around in the belly of a fish gives you time to think. It's a wake-up call, a chance to stop believing the delusion that you're in charge. Suffering and hardship can be like that—a chance to reevaluate our priorities and remember who is above the circumstances of life. It's not us, but it's easy to get drawn into thinking otherwise. Difficulties are a chance to reorient our devotion to the Lord and to experience his overwhelming love. In our selfishness and pride, we block our ability to receive it. Selfishness is the idolatry of self. It's an attitude that turns us from God and traps us in our circumstances.

Jonah's circumstances cause him to reevaluate, and with his change of perspective comes the end of his time inside the fish:

> *Those who cling to worthless idols*
> *turn away from God's love for them.*

> *But I, with shouts of grateful praise,*
>   *will sacrifice to you.*
> *What I have vowed I will make good.*
>   *I will say, 'Salvation comes from the Lord.'"*
> *And the Lord commanded the fish, and it vomited*
> *Jonah onto dry land. (Jonah 2:8-10)*

Rather than running from God and seeking his own preference, Jonah tells God he will sacrifice to him (Jon. 2:9). In other words, he's giving something up for God. It's a sign that things have changed, that his heart has conformed to reality, and that he knows who God is, finally. God is again at the center of things for Jonah. When his heart changes, his circumstances change.

Jonah offers up a shout of "grateful praise." It's hard to appreciate someone else when you're centered on yourself. When we find ourselves trapped in the belly of a whale—in hardship and in need of God's help—we must recognize we've gotten things wrong and allowed our priorities to wander. The solution is to let our selfish plans go and keep our commitment to God, just as Jonah did, trusting that he can rescue us from any situation. It may be that our self-centeredness and pride is what's keeping us from his salvation.

God is able to do anything. That means God is more powerful than anything we're facing. Nothing can resist his will or deter him from doing what's right. What we should want, in any situation, is that very thing—what's *right*. It's the solution that furthers his perfect plan. To that end, evil and suffering are necessary conditions in the world. They are opportunities for his power to be revealed. Any thought that something in the universe can resist God is mere confusion; his might is unstoppable, his judgment unquestionable, and his love unconditional. If this is the starting point for our lives, we view hardship in a completely different way than Jonah. We run toward his purposes, not away from them. We find within our difficulties a chance to know him as we never have before.

Knowing and Acknowledging Who God is

Saying something out loud is a good way to keep the truth in front of us. We learn to recite great truths for this reason. In the United States, reciting the Pledge of Allegiance and singing our national anthem cause us to remember essential truths about God, our commitment, and the courage our freedom is built upon. By proclaiming them, we keep the principles before us and don't take them for granted. We're bombarded with a lot of different ideas today; not all of them echo those same truths. We can combat the lies and delusions we're fed by a culture controlled by consumerism by reminding ourselves of what really matters.

We reflected on Nebuchadnezzar last chapter and how God broke his pride for his own good. In contrast to him is the man who delivered God's judgment, the prophet Daniel. Daniel knew God in a way that was profound and personal. God honored Daniel with the most revealing and profound insights into the future of his plan of any prophet in the Old Testament. God reveals his power over and over in this man's life. We see his humility and faith honored time and time again through the book, as he encounters hardship and disaster with an unyielding trust in God. But Daniel's heart is most clearly revealed by the way he prays, as described in Dan. 9.

In a study of the writings of Jeremiah, Daniel comes across God's promise to release Israel from its captivity in Babylon after seventy years. It had been precisely seventy years. He goes to prayer to ask God to keep his promise, but it's not *what* he asks that is so revealing. It's *how* he asks it. It's not just an example of how we should pray, but how we should approach life.

Daniel begins his prayer with the most important conviction in his life: "O Lord, the great and awesome God, who keeps his covenant of love with all who love him and obey his commands" (Dan. 9:4). God is great, awesome, and loving. God keeps his promises. There is no mindset here of blame on God, there is no doubt about God's faithfulness and love, and there is no uncertainty about God's ability to come through and rescue Israel from captivity. It is the beginning of this prayer because it is the starting point of everything in his life. It's the secret to his success. God is the sovereign God. He is awesome and great. He is not a genie who may or may not grant your wishes. He is faithful to his promises, which are rooted in his love.

A rabbi by the name of Harold Kushner wrote a book many years ago entitled *When Bad Things Hap-*

pen to Good People. Kushner's theory was that God was real and cared about us, but was prevented from acting in human history to change things. He was there to comfort you but could not help you. He could not influence tangible things in this world or in your life. Kushner writes,

> *I believe in God. But I do not believe the same things about Him that I did years ago, when I was growing up or when I was a theological student. I recognize His limitations. He is limited in what He can do by laws of nature and by the evolution of human nature and human moral freedom. ... I can worship a God who hates suffering but cannot eliminate it, more easily than I can worship a God who chooses to make children suffer and die, for whatever exalted reason.*

Kushner believes in God, but he doesn't know him. Not really. His God isn't powerful. He mistakenly concludes that God couldn't have a morally sufficient reason to permit suffering. It's a modern view that lets God off the hook for tragedy but leaves us with someone completely different than the God of the Bible. Daniel didn't know about that God. The God he knows is a God who can do anything. A God who acts not only within human history but within our lives. Who doesn't just comfort us when we face hardship but rescues people from the flames. He walks in the flames *with* us. He is a God who closes the mouths of lions to protect those who put their trust in him. That's Daniel's God.

The miraculous life that Daniel had wasn't a coincidence; it was a life built on knowing who God was and acknowledging it in all the encounters of life. But if we know who God is, we also know who we are, in comparison to him. Prayer is not only a moment when we proclaim who he is, but acknowledge who we are.

Knowing Ourselves and Accepting Our Failure

God can't support sin. He can't honor disobedience. His holiness prevents it. In Daniel's time, Israel is living with the consequences of its sin and lack of faith. Daniel acknowledges this in his prayer: "We have sinned and done wrong. We have been wicked and have rebelled; we have turned away from your commands and laws. We have not listened to your servants the prophets, who spoke in your name to our kings, our princes and our fathers, and to all the people of the land" (Dan. 9:5-6).

Daniel has a heart of accepting responsibility for his people's failure because he has a heart of accepting responsibility for his own failure. It's the second step in his prayer because it is the second fundamental posture of his life. If you really know who God is, then you also know who you are in relation to him. You are not God. He is powerful and holy and faithful, and—you're not. When you don't follow him, you suffer consequences in your life. That's not God's fault. That's your fault. When you put the first two components of this prayer together, who he is and who you are, what you have is a posture of worship, surrender, and repentance.

Daniel has this posture, so you see the back-and-forth contrasts he makes with God's righteousness on the one hand, and Israel's faithlessness on the other, in verses 7 and following. In Dan. 9:8 he says, "Open shame belongs to us, O Lord." Why? "Because we have sinned against you." That's quite an admission.

My life hasn't entirely worked out the way I'd hoped. I've gone through times when I was bitter and blamed God for not helping me. Times when I couldn't have prayed a prayer like Daniel's because I blamed God for my problems. We've all had disappointments in our lives. But here's a thing I've learned. It's something Daniel seems to have known his whole life: God is loving and holy, and to the degree I've missed out on his blessings, it is because I didn't obey him. He was there always, waiting for me, loving me, with a plan to redeem me despite my failure and stubbornness. Just like he waited for Israel for seventy years. This is our God.

God isn't looking for perfect people. Being perfect isn't the secret of Daniel's success. Daniel wasn't perfect. In Dan. 9:20 he not only acknowledges his people's sin but his own also. God is looking for repentant people. What is repentance? How do you repent?

It starts by looking in a mirror. Try it. Ask yourself a question: *Where am I rebelling?* You know you are. We all are. There is some lie you're living, some habit or desire that's taken you the wrong way, something you do to make yourself feel better that you know isn't right but you don't want to stop, so it's hard to face. I know because I'm just like you. We're all the same. The second stop on the way to experiencing God's power is to stare directly at whatever it is and confess it. *Lord, open shame belongs to me because I have sinned against you.* That is a very hard prayer to pray, especially in a culture that likes to put the blame on someone else. But that acknowledgment is the key to finding our way to the power God offers in the most difficult circumstances of life.

Controlled by the Little Things

If our picture of God is wrong, the disappointments in life control us. We react rather than look up at the one who is sovereign over all things. We scramble to find our own solution and experience relief, no matter what the cost or how great the compromise. We misinterpret the situation and doubt that God is in control.

As Paul writes to a church in Rome facing increased persecution, he develops an argument to reorient their thinking that can serve us also. In Rom. 8:31-32 he asks two rhetorical questions:

- *If God is for us, who can be against us?*
- *He who did not spare his own Son, but gave him up for us all—how will he not also, along with him, graciously give us all things?*

This is an argument from the larger to the smaller. Rather than focus on the little things and let them tell us who God is, we should start with the larger truth and let it guide our perspective on the little things. If the Creator of the universe is for you, who can be against you? The larger truth is that *God is for us*. He's not against us, and, in fact, if he's for us, *no one* can stand against us. No circumstances are so great they cannot be overcome.

The second question is similar. If God would suffer and die on a cross for you, would he refuse to give you everything you need in life? The larger truth is that Jesus died as an expression of God's love. The pain and disappointment you feel today doesn't mean you've been discarded or forgotten or that he doesn't have plans to bless you and save you. The big picture gives us an answer to all the little uncertainties we face in life.

We need to think from larger to smaller because we focus on the small things. The pain and challenges of the moment. When you lose the big picture of God's love, you are controlled by every little thing that goes wrong in your life.

Facing difficulties is like managing a difficult and dangerous mountain climb. Every time there is a crack that hurts your hands or some pebbles that fall down and bounce off your head, you change course, shifting and sliding, doing anything to feel a little better. Pretty soon you can find yourself isolated on a far ledge with no handholds above you and no way to go except down. The solution wasn't to avoid the difficulties of the climb. The solution was to fix your eyes on the top and keep going up.

We need to focus on the big picture, not the challenges of the moment. This is how alcohol addiction occurs, where you seek a quick fix to your pain and then it draws you into bigger problems. I once prayed for a lady who had an oxycodone addiction. She had legitimate pain at some point, but now she has more suffering because of drug withdrawals. She couldn't break free of it. This is also how affairs occur. Difficulties in your marriage go unresolved, and, in your hurt, you find an attractive person who seems to understand you. Then you become trapped in the sin and live with the consequences.

If you let the discouragements, pain, loss, disappointment, and loneliness control you, you *will* become stranded. The solution is to look up from the small struggles to see the big picture. Stop focusing on the problem in front of you and fix your eyes on him. God is there with his arms open. If he is for you, who can be against you? If he would not spare his own son, out of his love for you, how would he not graciously give you everything you need? In his timing, all things, even horrible things, work together for good.

Getting Your Just Deserts?

I grew up in a home where there was punishment for breaking the rules. One of the best things about growing up and moving out, in fact, was to live with impunity. Many of us grew up facing consequences for our behavior, whether helpful or overbearing, so we naturally look at difficulties in our life that way. Perhaps things are going wrong merely because we broke a rule. We envision God as a strict disciplinarian who slaps us on the wrist for our lack of perfection. He brings disaster as a way to enforce his rules and even the score.

This conception is one of the reasons that *karma* is such a popular idea today, even in Western societies. If tragedy is payback for mistakes we made in some previous life, we might find it easier to accept our hardship and move on. The problem for Christians, of course, is that we have only one life to live. We can't blame some earlier version of ourselves. So we're left with the conclusion that we made a mistake, only to have God's wrath raining down on us.

As we saw in the last section, Paul wrote to the church in Rome to reorient their thinking about the persecution they were facing. He goes on to ask two additional rhetorical questions in Rom. 8:33-34 to put to rest any concern that God was condemning them for doing something wrong. God has many reasons for permitting suffering in our lives, but condemnation isn't one of them. It's not payback. He doesn't need to bring us tragedy to even the score. He evened the score two thousand years ago by the death of his Son.

- *Who will bring any charge against those whom God has chosen?* It is God who justifies.
- *Who then is the one who condemns?* No one. Christ Jesus who died—more than that, who was raised to life—is at the right hand of God and is also interceding for us.

Whoever brings a charge against us, we know it isn't God. He justified us. *Justification* is the act of making us right in his sight. We experience that justification by faith in Christ. It is the work of an instant as we place our trust in him, made possible by an event—Christ's death—that happened millennia ago. Without a charge against us, there can't be a penalty—not one that stems from God's justice, in any case.

As a result, there is no one left to condemn us for our sin. That not only includes the sins we committed in the past but the mistakes we make in the present. As we confess them, Jesus continues to stand in our place. His death is sufficient to cover us. No punishment remains if we trust him.

I made a lot of mistakes, growing up. I have said things that have been hurtful and crossed lines I should not have. I was rude and disrespectful to my parents. I crashed my parents' car when I was 16, in fact. I don't remember if I said I was sorry—I probably didn't. My mom could go on and on about my mistakes. But because she loves me, none of that matters any longer. It is the same with God, out of his love for us. We are not defined by our past. I may live with consequences from my sin, but not condemnation.

God's Love

When get slammed by pain and tragedy, it sometimes feels like God disappears. We experience financial failure, and it feels like we have no help. Our health fails, or we endure the loss of someone we love, and we feel alone. It might seem like God doesn't care.

However you feel because of what you are going through, whether you are happy or sad, you can never be separated from the love of Jesus Christ. You may feel panicked, alone, uncertain, in despair, but you cannot lose his love. Your feelings don't matter. Nothing can block the plans that God has for your life. Those plans may lead you through some very difficult times, but they cannot be stopped. His love cannot be stopped.

In Rom. 8:35, Paul asks a final rhetorical question to put aside any doubt on the part of the Christians in Rome: *Who shall separate us from the love of Christ? Shall trouble or hardship or persecution or famine or nakedness or danger or sword?* Paul chooses these examples because they are elements in his own life. He faced trouble, hardship, persecution, famine, nakedness, danger, and the sword. That's *his* story. The fact that circumstances were often out of control, that he faced death constantly, might lend support to the thesis that something had gone wrong.

It's tempting in those times to think God's love has run out. It just happens to be false, and it suggests we don't know him or understand suffering correctly. Our victory over the harsh circumstances of life isn't always by being rescued from them. It's the power we receive in the midst of them. It's the strength he gives us to endure circumstances and not let them control us. Paul answers his own question this way: "No, in all these things we are more than conquerors through him who loved us" (Rom. 8: 37). The power we receive happens precisely because of these hardships. In receiving it, we emerge as conquerors, not as those defeated by the circumstances of life. We grow closer to the people we were meant to be, precisely because of the difficulties we face. But to see that, you have to recognize God's love and the purpose behind our lives.

The tragedies of life cannot separate us from God's love. However abandoned we feel by God, no hardship indicates that his love for us has changed. Not mistreatment by others, or the loss of possessions, or financial loss. Not the threat of physical harm, or anxiety and loneliness. The tangible challenges of life do not mean we have lost anything. His love cannot be stopped.

Hardship not only does *not* mean that God has abandoned us, but it is a sign that we are on his path. There is a powerful force for evil in this world. It stands in opposition to the cross of Christ. If I align myself with the Lord, I am part of a bigger struggle and I may have pain. But in the end, I will have victory, together with the Lord. All that matters is the end, not the difficulties along the way. In all these things, we are more than conquerors. God's plans are far beyond the struggles we face. We cannot lose, because the meaning of our lives is tied to his plans for all of creation. It is a story of love, and you are woven into it.

Our Destiny is Secure

Sometimes our journey is difficult. Like a trek to the

top of a mountain, we might forget that the difficulties are a necessary part of reaching the destination. Or in childbirth, where the pain is part of the process that results in something so wonderful. Our victory is that, no matter what this life throws at us, we are headed to the place we are meant to be, and nothing can stop it. Death isn't the end; it's the threshold to something greater. Even that final challenge is not a tragedy when we recognize what it means. It means hardship and loss did not define us. Suffering did not prevent us from reaching the destiny we were created for.

Death was the only threat the difficulties of life held over us, and that was broken by the love of God. Our path to him, however difficult, will lead us to where we were meant to be all along. Paul concludes Rom. 8 this way: "For I am convinced that neither death nor life, neither angels nor demons, neither the present nor the future, nor any powers, neither height nor depth, nor anything else in all creation, will be able to separate us from the love of God that is in Christ Jesus our Lord" (Rom. 8:38-39).

We are not yet at the end of the story; we're in between. But we know how it will end. Knowing the end draws us through whatever difficulties we face, whatever doubts plague us. The knowledge that we are known and loved transforms us. It carries us through the worst life throws at us and compels us to do great things in the time we are here—if we will trust God and keep our focus.

The Lord loves you. He has not abandoned you.

Whatever you face in life, whatever mistakes you have made, he stands before you with open arms. Nothing can separate you from that love or keep you from being the person he has made you to be. Nothing can block his plans for your life. It is a life that will go on forever if you have put your faith in him.

Chapter 6:
Power Made Perfect

One of the challenges in being a parent is knowing when to let your children struggle and when to step in and take control of things. There is a lesson in both responses. By allowing our children to wrestle with a problem and eventually find their way to a solution, we teach them to persevere and develop character through adversity. They'll never learn what their limits are if we rescue them from every difficulty in life. By stepping in at points when they truly need help, though, we teach them the value in relying on others. If we do it with compassion, we model the kind of loving response we hope will develop in their own lives as they encounter others who struggle.

I allow my children to rely on me in spite of our culture's emphasis on independence because one of the keys to fulfillment is found in trusting others and receiving love in return. That happens more rarely in a culture of self-centered individualism. But the truth is that our self-will is often the thing that keeps us from getting the help we need. My son can't reach out and grab hold of my hand unless he lets go of all the other things he's holding onto—all the alternatives he thinks will meet his needs. But in the embrace of a father who loves him, his needs will always be met.

It's the same for us. God is the most perfect example of a father, and he wants us to become the people he created us to be. To do so, we need to struggle through the circumstances of life and persevere. When we are overwhelmed, we need to trust in his love for us and not be afraid.

The power we have as human beings is illusory. Control is a figment of the imagination. We are all at the mercy of life. We have moments when we feel strong and capable, but they're transitory. The sense that we've got it under control is sometimes enough to keep us from reaching out to our Father, grabbing hold, and experiencing his power.

If we do, though, God is prepared to work through our lives in ways we can scarcely dream of. It's the goal of the Christian life and the purpose why we are here on earth. The problem is that almost everything in our culture is set up to keep us from experiencing God's power.

The Fruit of the Spirit

But the fruit of the Spirit is love, joy, peace, for-bearance, kindness, goodness, faithfulness, gentle-ness and self-control. Against such things there is no law.

Those who belong to Christ Jesus have crucified the flesh with its passions and desires. (Gal. 5:22-24)

We experience God's power the same way we do God's life. It comes from trusting him in a way that makes us capable of receiving it. So the path to power isn't found wherever we happen to take ourselves. It comes by walking with him in the direction he's heading. To head along that path means living a holy life. It comes by agreeing with the destination he's determined, not necessarily the one that makes sense to us. We find our way along his path and realize the power he offers us, by becoming the people we are meant to be.

There is a common misconception that Christiani-ty is about restrictions, about not being allowed to do what we want. It has been associated with puritanical morals and a hypocritical emphasis on rules and reg-ulations. It's an unfortunate way to look at the Chris-tian life. Christianity is about a life lived in pursuit of everything we are meant to be. It's about freedom from the things that prevent the joy and peace we long for. As Christians, we're not trying to be perfect as some puritanical ideal, but to be *complete*.

Achieving a complete life is a process we're led

through by the Spirit of God. It's not a limitation of our behavior so much as a transformation of our desires and tendencies. It's not pressure to live by certain rules but the behavior that naturally accompanies the goal we're headed toward.

Paul calls the characteristics of that life the *fruit of the Spirit*. These are the experiences that emerge from a life lived under the guidance of the Holy Spirit, who produces within us the characteristics of the life we were meant to have. It's the same way an apple comes from a tree that bears apples, or grapes from a vine that bears grapes. The fruit is what the branch or the vine is meant to bring forth. The fruit is an extension of its life. Grapes are not some alien appendage or burden to the vine; they are the expression of its true purpose. What appears unnatural is a vine that has no grapes on it. Gnarled and barren, it is less than what it could be. But in the harvest, after months of proper care, we see its potential realized. It's the same with our lives.

Love, joy, and peace are the fruit of a life lived under the control of the Holy Spirit. We were intended to bear them as characteristics of our lives. Unsurprisingly, they are things the world is trying to strip away from us at every turn. Bound as we are by the demands of our culture, we don't have the lives we're meant to have. We deal with anxiety and stress on a daily basis. As we try to control circumstances and distract ourselves from the things that cause us pain, we wither and shrink. We're barren vines in arid soil. We produce something other than the fruit we're meant for—like the weeds and insects that prolifer-ate vines left untended. We live our lives in neglect of the purposes for which we were created. We think it's too much work. But holiness isn't a chore; it's the only way to realize the kind of life we need and were made to have.

We reach the goal of the harvest by following the Holy Spirit. Like a parent, God directs us in a path to true life. But he leaves it to us to follow his lead. Fol-lowing God in the middle of a world opposed to his values requires trust. It's the reason why we're here, and why so few make the journey. Trust is *faith*, viewed in active terms. It's really the only definition of faith that the New Testament knows about, though James allows for something less than active faith when he writes, "Faith by itself, if it is not accompa-nied by action, is dead" (James 2:17). Some transla-tions use the word *works* to describe the action he's speaking of, but the NIV captures the idea correctly. Active faith is different than mere cognition. It's more than an idea. You can think about something all you want, but if it doesn't affect your behavior, there's no power in it. That kind of faith is no more than a pass-ing thought.

Following the Spirit happens not in spite of the challenges of life but because of them. As we face sit-uations that offer us the chance to choose between God's will and our own way, we have the chance to follow him and be changed. We take steps toward the lives we want. We become people that his power can dwell within and shine through. We become *vessels that hold his power.*

The fruit of the Spirit is love, joy, and peace, to name a few. These are not just ideas or emotional states but behaviors. People who have *love* as a fruit of the Spirit are one and the same people who sacrifice for others. They aren't people who necessarily have an emotional experience called love; they are people who can't help but deny themselves and put other people's needs first. They act in sacrificial ways that are a natural extension of who they are and who they are increasingly becoming, under the guidance of the Spirit of God. Those actions are the very definition of love.

Similarly, people who have *joy* as a fruit of the Spirit aren't necessarily happy people. Happiness is a transitory emotional state. Joy is far more. Joy can lead you through the most difficult circumstances of life with a sense of fulfillment that nothing else can touch. It is present and powerful in precisely those moments when you are least likely to be happy. Similarly, *peace*, as a fruit of the Spirit, is not the serenity so many long for but the certainty your Father will never abandon you. It's the kind of peace you need when things are most out of control, when mere serenity fails by definition. You don't see love, joy, and peace of this kind in the world at large—quite the opposite. Worry, anxiety, cruelty, animosity, and manipulation are the standard. Addiction and conflict reign. Drug use is on the rise to offset the pain of not having the fruit of the Spirit in our lives. Our culture has no answers for the emptiness so many struggle with. We nonetheless pursue a cultural solution to our pain and end up further than ever from the kind of life we need.

In the challenges of life, in our suffering and disappointment, a way always presents itself to meet our needs through some cultural shortcut. We refer to these as *temptations*, but let's set that term aside because we use it to describe a lot of good things that we want but know we should avoid, like chocolate cake. Chocolate cake isn't bad in and of itself; every so often, you can indulge if you exercise and eat healthy food. The world's solutions to our pain aren't that kind of temptation. They are things that only hurt us, no matter how hard we try to counterbalance them with positive behavior. The world offers us solutions that are in opposition to relying on God. They are substitutes for what we need, not extra calories we can work off later. In accepting cultural substitutes for the fruit of the Spirit, we find ourselves further from the life we want and everything we were created to be.

Drugs aren't to be avoided simply because they're dangerous; they're to be avoided because they block you from achieving your purpose. They trap you in a mindset that is harmful, a reliance on something that is robbing you of the love, joy, and peace you desperately need. You not only don't get those by using drugs, you almost certainly guarantee you'll never have them. There's no room for the fruit of the Spirit in a life controlled by addiction. The fruit of the Spirit is not compatible with that kind of life.

So as a first step, choose reliance on God. He leads you to the alternative that is best for you. It's the less-flashy, less immediate resolution to your pain, but the one that will take you a step closer to the person you need to be. His path is often through the middle of your struggle, not around it. But in the journey, you emerge differently than when you began. You gain something. In time, you will change. You will be more yourself than when you started. And, you will be ready to receive his power.

We don't see God working as powerfully in our culture because fewer of us have done what I'm describing and what Paul commends in his writings. It's too easy now to become caught up in an addiction. Sex, substances, pornography, video games—the list grows as technology extends our ability to choose an expedient cultural solution to our pain and emptiness. Discipleship becomes harder and more elusive, the more often we do. But the path to the life you want starts from where you're standing right now, and it's not as far away as you might suspect.

Vessels of Power and Glory

One of the goals of consumer culture is to always be *full*. We fill ourselves with many things: activities, careers, transportation, relationships, technology. Today's media guarantees we have endless content. We don't just stuff ourselves with what's good; we indulge in celebrities and lifestyle pursuits, earning as much as we can to fill our time and keep ourselves ready for the next big thing. We aim for sensory overload. Mobile phones (soon to be be known simply as *phones*) guarantee we're always plugged-in. We think the more we have, the better life is. One more thing, then another, then another. There's always something else we need, it seems like, and never enough time or money to get it. When difficulties hit, they hurt even more because we view losses as entirely negative. We never consider that the failure of a relationship or inability to pursue our favorite pastime might be good for us, that we're not meant for an overload. But a loss can provide the freedom we need to achieve our potential.

A cup overflowing with mud has no room for wine in it, and mud is in cheap supply. What we need isn't for God to top us off with just a little pour of wine, because any amount of wine mixed into a cup of mud results in more mud. Wine + mud = mud. What we need first is to become *empty*. As empty vessels, we are ready to receive whatever he has for us and experience it completely.

Difficulties can eliminate what prevents us from receiving the kind of life he created us for. Some years ago, I lost my business. That same year, I lost my home, and shortly after that, I lost my wife to divorce. As I struggled to understand where God was at in the midst of it all, the thought I couldn't wrap my head around, at the time, was that my losses left me in a condition where the Spirit could fill me. What I eventually came to recognize was that my business, home, and even my marriage were not bad in themselves, but each of them, in different ways, had supplanted the presence of God in my life. By my own power and choice, I wouldn't have made the decisions necessary to correct what was wrong and draw close to God. But by the loss of these things, regardless of the failure involved in their departure, I found myself empty enough to receive what I'd been missing and desperately needed.

From my current vantage point back on everything that happened, these losses were necessary. My life was on a crash course. I was a prisoner of my pride, unable to see anything other than what I thought would make me happy. The Lord allowed me to be broken so that I could be healed. It is difficult to imagine that God has a positive end to tragedy when your dreams are falling apart. But it's this vision that God desires for all of us—that even the most cherished pursuits are worthless if they stand between who we are and who God has created us to be. His willingness to permit the loss of those things, however horrible and painful, can be an act of mercy when the loss permits him to fill us with something greater.

As disciples, we can spare ourselves some of this by voluntarily emptying ourselves of things that distract us from his purposes in our lives. When Paul writes in Phil 3:8, "What is more, I consider everything a loss because of the surpassing worth of knowing Christ Jesus my Lord, for whose sake I have lost all things," he isn't just talking about a way of thinking. He not only *considers* everything a loss compared to the surpassing worth of knowing Christ, he *actually lost* the things that stood in the way. The things he once valued—the things everyone else considered so great—he abandoned. We don't know the complete details of his losses; his younger life is still something of a mystery. But we know that the loss of those things allowed him to be used powerfully by God. He never looked at the exchange with regret; in Paul's mind, there was no comparison. It can be the same for you.

Perfectly You

It's hard for us to imagine we can become more authentically ourselves by giving things up, but it's true. We live in a society where we think our identity is created by piling more on. We *are* the cars we drive, the makeup and clothing we wear. But if you really cake it on, whatever it is, you're hiding, not becoming more authentic. Consumer culture delivers the delusion that we need to hide behind externals. We come to feel most comfortable when we're under the cloak of privacy. Transparency to others is frightening. But God sees us as we really are and loves us. Behind the trappings of prosperity, "coolness," sexiness, or our sense of humor, hides the person we truly are, however flawed. God loves us so much that he sometimes strips us down, removing the veneer we hide behind so that we can find our way to our true selves, away from the false identity our culture helps us create.

If we think of God's action as discipline—i.e., the intentional use of difficulties to push us in a direction that's good for us—we can find meaning in hardship. We can also realize a motivating response to the difficulties we face. We begin by asking ourselves questions. *Am I hiding? Have I surrounded myself with a false identity? If it is taken away, can I become something greater than I am right now?*

We don't normally think to ask these questions when things are falling apart, but they're critical to getting back on course, and perhaps the quickest way to getting through whatever we're facing. The idea that a loss can result in a gain is countercultural but it's true, and we see it happen all the time. It's a fact of life that little of value emerges that doesn't involve some degree of discipline.

As parents, enforcing discipline is one of the ways we help our children find their way to maturity and authenticity. We're only able to discipline them effectively (i.e., in a way that leads to a healthy result) if we know who they are. They're not deceivers, troublemakers, and rebels. If they were, we may as well lock them up and throw away the key. They're simply in the same process of growth as the rest of us. But we have a vision of them, not only who they are now, but who they may become. Discipline is something we use to help them reach their potential.

Discipline is also how an athlete stays in condition. If he or she gets out of shape, discipline is how they return to the condition necessary to compete. Implicit is the idea that being that kind of person—one who is ready to meet their potential—is not just good but essential. Anything else is settling for less than what we're built for.

In Hebrews 12, the author urges us to view things

in these simple terms: "Endure hardship as discipline; God is treating you as his children. For what children are not disciplined by their father? If you are not disciplined—and everyone undergoes discipline—then you are not legitimate, not true sons and daughters at all" (Heb. 12:7-8). When he says to "endure hardship as discipline," he means we should interpret the difficulties we go through as a process that God intends for our benefit. The goal is the same as for our own children—to become the kind, loving, faithful, honest, and self-controlled people we are meant to be. By urging us to endure, the author is suggesting we not look for the quickest way out, if that undermines the process God has us in for our own good. Not all hardship is inherently good for us, but we can become good as we face it as an exercise of faith. We need to sit with it and think, *God, show me how this can help me. What needs to change in my life? Am I trusting something instead of you?*

The author also makes the point that any loving father disciplines his children. If life goes smoothly no matter what values we hold and decisions we make, it's a sign that God isn't invested in our well-being. A loving parent can't stand idly by while their child destroys their life. God is no different. If he doesn't permit our selfish plans to succeed, it may be for our own good. He may allow our road to be bumpy because there is something more important than a smooth ride. We have a destiny beyond this life. Discipline is what helps us persevere to reach the finish line.

In Proverbs 12:1, Solomon writes, "Whoever loves discipline loves knowledge, but whoever hates correction is stupid." I've been stupid in my reaction to God's discipline at points in my life. But by his grace, he didn't bail me out at the moment I asked. He taught me to let go of the things that were hurting me. The life that emerged was the one I couldn't have found on my own. The trick is to see difficult times for what they are from the outset. Not to give in to fear or bitterness but to acknowledge God's sovereignty and purposes. If you can, you are mere steps from the power that lies at the core of the Christian life.

Glory in Sufferings

Paul found his way to a place of power. He saw every persecution, beating, shipwreck, and prison sentence as a chance to realize an even greater work of the Spirit in his life. In Rom. 5 he writes,

> *Not only so, but we also glory in our sufferings, because we know that suffering produces perseverance; perseverance, character; and character, hope. And hope does not put us to shame, because God's love has been poured out into our hearts through the Holy Spirit, who has been given to us. (Rom. 5:3-5)*

Paul is tracking the purpose behind suffering, viewed as discipline. He was committed not only to developing proven character for its own sake, but because of what it led to. Those who suffer, persevere, and develop character are ready for the out-working of God's power. He uses the word *hope* to refer to what emerges from character, but this word can be confusing in English. *Hope* is often a vague yearning for something, in today's usage. It might represent no more than an irrational wish. We might say, "I hope my lottery ticket wins the big jackpot." At the longest possible odds, that doesn't say very much about the quality of my hope. But this isn't what Paul means in Romans 5. Hope is an *anticipation* of some-thing certain. It's the rational expectation that God would reveal himself in the life of someone who fol-lowed the path he described—through suffering and perseverance, to the development of character. Our hope is the anticipation that God will work powerful-ly through our suffering.

Character is not something that comes from a few casual decisions but the transformation that occurs within us because we trust God in the middle of our struggles, over and over. In the end, we change. We become the people we're meant to be—faithful, joy-ful, loving, and holy. When we do, something else happens. Paul writes of it: We anticipate God's power through the Holy Spirit. We can expect it because God has already revealed his love to us through the Spirit. That same Spirit produces an outworking of a power we rarely see and can scarcely understand in today's world.

Miracle

We live in a world where the idea of miracles is ridiculed. Science (or more accurately, *scientism*) has told us that only things in the natural world are real, that reality is bound by the limits of our five senses. Scientism isn't just the view that we can only know the world through our senses; it's the presupposition that only what we can see, smell, taste, touch, and hear is real. Anything that science can't measure is *unreal*. It *can't* be true if it can't be measured. It's nothing more than fantasy. But this presupposition itself is a fallacy. Why should we believe it? It can't be proven using the five senses. It's an idea about what is true that, applied to itself, is disqualified from being true. It's a leap of faith, a self-contradiction. But it's proliferated by our educational system. It's the default presupposition of Western culture. It's out of line with human experience. It also happens to be false.

If God created the reality we experience—the physical world, time, space, and our minds—he can do anything he likes with respect to the physical universe, as long as it's not in contradiction to his nature. He can heal people of illness, bring people back to life, feed thousands of people with a few pieces of bread and fish, and walk on water. These things are easy for him. Scientism doesn't deny them because they're impossible. A miracle isn't something impossible. A miracle is *an effect in the physical world caused by an agent who is non-physical.* The creation of the universe from nothing is a miracle, under this definition. It might appear impossible, but all we mean is that we can't explain it, based on human agency and physical causes. Science can discuss the creation of the physical universe (and does, as the *Big Bang Theory*), but it can't explain *how* or *why* it happened. The fact that science can't explain it doesn't mean a miracle didn't happen. The world around us is evidence of that miracle.

With technology, we can accomplish many feats that would have once been considered miraculous. But these are wonders, not miracles, because the cause is located in the physical realm. Science denies miracles because they originate in God, and God isn't himself in the physical realm and therefore cannot exist, according to scientism. But the existence of God is the point under consideration. Is God real? Does he love us? Can he help us when things go wrong? If he exists, then miracles are not only possible but are, in a sense, expected. If so, we still don't know why we don't see them more often, especially when we need help. But that's the very point we're exploring. If miracles occur in the context of a certain kind of life, and our culture propels us away from that life, we don't expect to see miracles happen very often. The secret to experiencing God's power in our lives is to have the kind of life conducive to an outworking of that power.

In a culture that tells us to trust ourselves, do whatever we want, deny God, indulge our sexuality, and pursue superficial happiness at the expense of proven character, we can't expect the miraculous. Miracles don't normally develop in the content of those priorities. Stories of the miraculous trickle in from the mission field but are elusive here in the U.S. and are virtually nonexistent in Europe. We don't approach life in a way that allows for God's power to become manifest through our lives.

It's a conundrum because Jesus promised in John 14:12, "Very truly I tell you, whoever believes in me will do the works I have been doing, and they will do even greater things than these, because I am going to the Father." If we look around today, we might be tempted to think Jesus had it wrong, but it's only because we confuse his point. The belief he is talking about is not Christianity as a religion or social custom. He makes it more clear in v. 15 when he equates worship with something other than casual religious observance: "If you love me, keep my commands." The powerful life is the life that perseveres. It obeys when things get most difficult. It aligns itself with God's purposes and reflects his holiness. God works powerfully and miraculously in the context of the belief exhibited by that kind of life. A life spent in pursuit of self, controlled by sin and focused on the dream of personal success, is headed in precisely the opposite direction.

In contrast, a life that faces adversity and turns to God has the potential to receive his power. It is a chance to be used powerfully and to see God work miraculously. Jesus's promise in John 14:12 wasn't limited to the apostolic age; it's a guarantee to anyone who trusts him. It has been true for all people in the years since he spoke it. And it has the same potential in your life also. But any outworking of his power, small or great, is dependent on us. If we refuse to become the people we are meant to be, we will experience little of this, despite God's desire to reveal his power and work through us for his glory.

Hardship is one path to the outworking of the miraculous for the very reason that it provides the opportunity for us to show the kind of trust Jesus is talking about. It's like a wind-tunnel—a storm that is specially created to test the airplane's ability to fly. It's a proving ground. It's not a simulation but the most extreme conditions, amplified to test our beliefs and measure our response. It was the same for Jesus Christ, who was perfected through his suffering (Heb. 2:10). Hardship can help us reach the point where we are forced to change to sustain the pain we face. We develop proven character and are emptied of the things that control us. We become entirely reliant on God. And in so doing, we exhibit the fruit of a life he can work through.

God's gifts and calling are at his discretion, not available on demand. But they don't appear irrespective of who we are and how we live. If we want to see God work through us in any measure, we must submit to a process. We must be emptied of the things our culture has pressed on us. We have to trust God and walk with him in holiness. We have to follow Jesus and stay on his path. What happens, if we do, depends on our calling. God created each of us uniquely to serve him in different ways, and his power manifests accordingly. But the degree to which we experience miracles in our lives is purely a consequence of the part he chooses for us in his plan. If your heart and mind are drawn to his service, and you experience the transformation of the Holy Spirit in the core of your life, even mountains can move.

Expectation of Power

I came to you in weakness with great fear and trembling. My message and my preaching were not with wise and persuasive words, but with a demonstration of the Spirit's power, so that your faith might not rest on human wisdom, but on God's power. (1 Cor. 2:3-5)

But I will come to you very soon, if the Lord is willing, and then I will find out not only how these arrogant people are talking, but what power they have. For the kingdom of God is not a matter of talk but of power. (1 Cor. 4:19-20)

In Western culture, we've stopped expecting God to work powerfully. We put him in a box and think we need to take control of circumstances using our own resources and by our own strength. We think miracles are stories for children and the superstitious, and our ministries are focused on self-help rather than reliance on God. As we look around, we can't help but notice that Christianity is very similar to the culture we live in, focused on a pursuit of individual happiness and Hollywood's definition of fulfillment. We shouldn't be surprised to see so little power in the church today. As a result, very little of Christianity in Western culture resembles the Christianity of the first two centuries. When Paul speaks of power in his letter to the Corinthians, he doesn't just associate it with his ministry specifically but with the kingdom of God generally. He doesn't speak of it as the exception, but as the basis for validating the message being delivered. Christianity isn't just about a message but a *transformation* that occurs when our words are backed by God's power.

Paul roots the power behind his ministry in a work of the Holy Spirit (2 Cor. 2:6-16). He removes any suggestion that it is derived from his own capabilities by emphasizing his own weakness (1 Cor. 2:3). Our weakness, accompanied by a manifestation of God's power in and through our lives, is the combination we've been discussing. It's an expectation that Paul mentions to the church in Corinth as a way to disqualify the false teaching they've been hearing. The Spirit of God is powerful, then and now. Lives change in connection with the word of God being proclaimed in truth and in power. But the stumbling block, then, is the same as today. Our strength interferes with an outworking of the Holy Spirit.

We don't let go of the things that stand in the way of God revealing his glory and power. We increasingly embrace them in our lives and in our ministries, believing that a flashy and polished show will draw more people into our churches. As individuals, we cling to the things that make us appear prosperous and attractive. We depend on ourselves as the basis for how we live and the ministry we offer others. But God won't have any of that. It's not the context for the

gospel. It's an impediment. It should come as no surprise, then, when God has mercy on us and allows
hardship to overcome us as a method of discipline.
He wants more for us than the emptiness and insig-
nificance we're willing to settle for.

The path back for the church in Western culture is
the same as for each of us who yearns to see God reveal his power and presence in our lives: We need to
let go of what we're trusting in and grab onto him,
with every fiber of our being. We need to walk along
the path Jesus left for us and center our lives on the
same values. That path will lead us to the one who
created us. But it's not simply for the destination that
we walk it, but for the journey itself. Along the way,
there is power in his service. Each step in the journey
has its own measure of peace, joy, and love.

The Secret of Being Content

> *I am not saying this because I am in need, for I
> have learned to be content whatever the circum-
> stances. I know what it is to be in need, and I know
> what it is to have plenty. I have learned the secret
> of being content in any and every situation,
> whether well fed or hungry, whether living in
> plenty or in want. I can do all this through him
> who gives me strength. Phil. 4:11-13*

I try to avoid watching commercials; it's pretty easy
now, with digital recorders and services like Netflix. I
remember when I first bought a Tivo. The biggest ex-
citement for me wasn't the ability to schedule

recording. What I loved was that I could fast forward through commercials. They bug me, and they exist purely to convince me to buy something, which also bugs me. Commercials have no other purpose than that: to create some sense of emptiness or neediness which can be fulfilled by purchasing the product in question.

In our culture, advertising gets results because we're all looking for something. It's either the hope of happiness or the promise of personal success. We feel like we'd be happier if we lost a few pounds, had whiter teeth, or had a more expensive car to drive. It's hard to know if, over the history of Western culture, advertising is the very reason why we feel that way (if it's changed the way we think of life), or if advertising exists as a response to some other cultural pressure. It's probably some of both. Consumer society makes us empty, makes us feel like we need things, and provides a solution that meets our needs, but only temporarily.

In John 4, Jesus encounters a Samaritan woman at a well in a desert village, in the heat of the day. He tells her that if she drinks of the water from that well, she will thirst again, but if she drinks of the living water—the water only he can provide—she will never be thirsty. This is how it is with the things of this world: they satisfy us for a bit, but we always need more. What God offers us is something that will satisfy us forever, if we will drink of it. It is the thing that Paul mentions in Phil. 4:12, the secret to be learned. The secret he learned. The secret we also can learn.

We can get through any and every situation in life by placing our cares into the hands of our God, trusting that he is in control. He provides us the strength to endure any circumstance we face. We don't need the temporary relief that this world provides.

He is enough.

At times of extreme pain and hardship, it's difficult to remember that. I have been through some times where I couldn't bear how much pain I had, and anything that could make me feel better, even for a short while, sounded good to me. The end result, just like buying things to fill the void inside of us, is just more emptiness when the temporary relief fades away.

Paul sits in prison as he writes Philippians. Circumstances were not looking up for him. The precise nature of his imprisonment is debated among scholars, but the words of this book speak of the greatest joy, purpose, and love for Christ in the middle of hardship of any book in the Bible. I want to be like this man, when I face the challenges and discouragements of life.

Over the years it's become easier, but I have to admit, it's only because of long, painful times when things were not going well for me. I had no choice but to turn to God; nothing else worked. He planned it that way. He needed me to learn the secret. That's the way Paul learned it. When you face difficult times and trust him, it becomes increasingly easier to do so. I am not sure there is any other way to learn the secret than facing hardship, but it is certainly the case that we can suffer and choose *not* to trust him. You must view the circumstances of your life as an opportunity to give your cares to him, release your fears, and experience his peace. He provides you the strength that you need. No meds are needed, no alcohol, no frivolous distractions. He is enough.

The Spirit of God is here, and he wants to transform your life also. Follow his leading. He wants to bring about peace and love in your life. He wants to lift you above the concerns you're facing and fill you with his joy.

Chapter 7:
Deep Wounds

When we experience hardship and disappointment, it's always something specific. It ranges the spectrum from losing something valuable or having our car break down to real tragedy, including the loss of someone we love or a serious illness. All of these are opportunities to trust God and see him work powerfully in our lives, but in extreme cases, we need extra help. We question God's love or wonder how we should respond, and we search the scriptures for more direction. It's difficult to be still and trust God in the most extreme difficulties we face. What God wants to do in your life is more important than the circumstances you face, but it is the case that he often wants us to learn something more than simply to trust him.

In this short chapter, I will briefly survey some of life's most significant losses. You might have faced these in the past, but it's likely you will face at least some of them in the future or know someone else who will. If so, God wants you to know that he is powerful and present.

Death of Someone You Love

When I was in my twenties, I returned home after being away on a trip and out of communication to learn that one of my best friends had been in a car accident. She was on the way to perform at a church event when a truck collided with her minivan. She and two of her kids were fine, as was the babysitter who was riding with them. Only Lynnie, her five-year-old daughter, had been hurt by the impact. She was killed instantly. When I heard the news, I rushed to her home to find a lot of friends gathered. The details of the accident were explained to me as I sat there, stunned. I didn't have questions about the crash. I had questions about why Lynnie had to die.

I can't put into words the impact this had on me. I'd spent a lot of time with Lynnie. My friend initially asked me to watch her kids while she performed at church that day, and I would have accepted if I weren't out of town. *I* should have been the babysitter, seated in the van when the accident happened. Lynnie wasn't my daughter, but I had lost something precious to me. Her death didn't make sense. She had

121

her entire life ahead of her.

All of a sudden, a troubling thought came to mind. None of this needed to happen. God could have stopped it. My resentment started to grow, and I found myself pulling away from the Lord.

My friend, however, drew close to him. She trusted in God's sovereignty and looked forward to the day she would see her daughter again. As I continued to doubt, Lynnie's mom drew strength from the Lord to continue on. The loss of her daughter opened doors for her to share her testimony with other parents who had lost their children.

In time things settled with me. But a crack had been opened in my faith. I doubted God's goodness.

In the years since then I've had other disappointments, but none that defied explanation like the death of this little girl. For years, I let it keep me from trusting God the way I should. That might be, in part, because of who I am. I am a rational person, a problem-solver. I make my living solving problems in technology. I've always found a certain degree of peace by fitting the pieces of a puzzle together. The tragedy of Lynnie's death was no different. It wasn't until I understood myself better that I found the answer I was looking for.

We can gain insight into trusting God with the loss of someone we love by studying John 11. In this chapter, Jesus's friend Lazarus gets sick and dies in a village several days journey from the place Jesus was staying when he is notified. Jesus understands that, in the tragedy, the Father intends to teach Lazarus's family and friends something important. And indirectly, of course, God shows us something as well. Jesus delays his departure to the village—not to let his friend die (his friend was too far away to reach in time, regardless) but to ensure his body would be entombed for three days by the time of his arrival. Many Jews believed the spirit of the deceased remained near the body for up to three days. By arriving after this, no one would question that Lazarus was beyond human intervention. It's the same lesson we've been discussing: In our weakness and inability lies the opportunity for God's power.

> *When Mary reached the place where Jesus was and saw him, she fell at his feet and said, "Lord, if you had been here, my brother would not have died."*
>
> *When Jesus saw her weeping, and the Jews who had come along with her also weeping, he was deeply moved in spirit and troubled. "Where have you laid him?" he asked.*
>
> *"Come and see, Lord," they replied.*
>
> *Jesus wept.*
>
> *Then the Jews said, "See how he loved him!"*
>
> *But some of them said, "Could not he who opened the eyes of the blind man have kept this man from dying?" (John 11:32-37)*

Some of those present were grumbling. Their words sound like things I've said in the middle of my own problems. *Lord, couldn't you have fixed my problems? Healed me? Resolved my financial issues? Saved my marriage? Prevented the loss of my home? Rescued a little girl from death?* I've asked these questions because I've expected God to make my dreams come true. And when he hasn't, sometimes, I've been bitter. Instead of trusting him, I miss the bigger picture, which is not based on my dreams, but his. His purposes don't always lead to the result we want, but they do point to a permanent solution—a coming kingdom—greater than all the tragedies of life.

If we accept that and stop looking for explanations for everything that goes wrong, we find a resolution, but not because we have answers. Answers don't always make sense in light of our limited knowledge, and sometimes the solution doesn't show itself until long after our suffering has ended. What we receive instead is *joy*. Joy is being lifted above the circumstances of life, into the arms of a Father who loves us and won't let us go. It's a rush to a high altitude, an experience beyond our cares and concerns. As children, we can't always see and understand. But we can experience the reassurance that he cares about our pain, just as we see in Jesus's response to his friend's death, even though Jesus knows the outcome of this tragedy. Our joy in combination with his compassion is enough, if we will trust him. The circumstances of this life are not a problem to be solved; they are an opportunity for God to reveal his power and his love.

Jesus said to her, "Your brother will rise again."

Martha answered, "I know he will rise again in the resurrection at the last day."

Jesus said to her, "I am the resurrection and the life. The one who believes in me will live, even though they die; and whoever lives by believing in me will never die. Do you believe this?"

"Yes, Lord," she replied, "I believe that you are the Messiah, the Son of God, who is to come into the world." (John 11:23-27)

Jesus says he is the *resurrection* and the *life*. The one who believes in him will live even though he dies—that's the *resurrection*. And whoever lives by believing in me, he says, will never die. That's the *life*. Jesus is saying that he is both the power that causes dead bodies to come to life, as well as the life that fills living people that carries them through death. The life you receive by believing in him will never end. That life begins today. It's the same life you and I receive as we trust in Jesus Christ. It will carry us through the worst things life can bring and into his arms. It's the life Lynnie had, and she is now in his loving hands.

God knows our pain as we confront tragedy and wait on him. He shares our sorrow for the results of sin and what it has done to our lives. God knows about your heartache. He also knows about the victory that is waiting for you, in the end. The certainty of what lies ahead can carry us through the greatest of life's tragedies if we will trust him.

Harm Caused by Others

The hardship we face at the hands of someone else can be the most difficult to manage. When we've been wronged, we have a direct target—someone we can blame for our pain and disappointment. It can be harder to allow God to work through that kind of circumstance than any other for the simple reason that we can identify the source. Our rage can take over and undermine the work of the Spirit in our lives. What often emerges from our lives are the very attitudes God intends to strip away (see Gal. 5:20).

When we are hurt by someone, we often lash out verbally. We have a tendency to label someone as *all bad*, and when we do that, it is often more than just a label. It can be an all-out verbal assault, where we vent our pain at the person's expense, either to their face or behind their backs to other people. We can be cruel and harsh, feeling justified because we have been damaged by them. It can feel like justice, to reveal the truth about what they did to hurt you. It might even be the case that what we're saying is true.

The issue isn't justice or truth. The issue is what we allow to fill our hearts.

I was hurt by someone. At the time, I felt like it was intentional. I couldn't keep silent. I let them have it, verbally. I thought they deserved it. But I was acting out of a wrong heart. I was refusing to listen to God. You may have had a similar experience, confronted with some deep pain, and found yourself responding verbally. If you haven't been hurt that badly yet, you may be one day.

In Matthew 12, Jesus responds to a group of Pharisees who are accusing him of being empowered by Satan:

> *"For the mouth speaks what the heart is full of. A good man brings good things out of the good stored up in him, and an evil man brings evil things out of the evil stored up in him. But I tell you that everyone will have to give account on the day of judgment for every empty word they have spoken. For by your words you will be acquitted, and by your words you will be condemned." Matt 12:34b-37*

Jesus's confrontation with the Pharisees is a direct challenge to his ministry. It would be easy to interpret the context of his words too narrowly and miss the general point: *What comes out of our mouths is a reflection of what is going on inside of us.* However justified we feel over the words we say, however wronged we have been by others, God has no part in rage, bitterness, and payback. If we think God is in support of harsh words, whether true or not, we are very mistaken. This kind of response is antithetical to the work of the Holy Spirit.

I remember hearing a sermon on these words, and I don't think I have ever felt more convicted in a church service. Not only because of things I have said but by the knowledge that, by not controlling my words, my heart was far from where it should have been. God wants me to turn my pain over to him and not try to relieve it by unloading verbally. He wants me to trust that he is in control and will make all things right. It is not my right to make someone suffer for their actions. God wants me to offer others the same mercy he has shown me.

It takes discipline to keep our mouths closed, sometimes. At the root of it all is our pain. We think that our words will correct wrongs and bring justice. We believe condemning others will make us feel better. Instead, we inflict on others the pain we experience ourselves, and in the process, allow that pain to become more deeply rooted in our hearts. Keeping silent or speaking graciously is not just what God wants for us; it is part of acknowledging that he is in control. It is a necessary step in having lives that honor him and reflect his goodness. It allows God to bring healing and transformation to our hearts. In withholding condemning words, we not only let go of those who have hurt us, we also let go of the past. It is the first step to being set free.

The second step is forgiveness.

When they kept on questioning him, he straightened up and said to them, "Let any one of you who is without sin be the first to throw a stone at her." Again he stooped down and wrote on the ground. At this, those who heard began to go away one at a time, the older ones first, until only Jesus was left, with the woman still standing there. Jesus straightened up and asked her, "Woman, where are they? Has no one condemned you?" "No one, sir," she said. "Then neither do I condemn you," Je-

sus declared. "Go now and leave your life of sin."
John 8:7-11

We all carry things. Pressure, stress, fear of the future. We allow things to burden us, and to the degree we do, we find ourselves dragged down, emotionally; we are held captive by our thoughts. We cannot avoid life's challenges or the horrible things that happen to us, but we can choose to let things take over and occupy our minds, or we can release those things and find peace in the Lord.

The stone that you carry, it weighs you down.

One of the biggest burdens we carry is the sense that someone has wronged us. It's not just the consequences that we bear, it is the wound left behind. It is the knowledge that someone did not value us enough to care for us. The greatest of this pain comes from people we have put our trust in. If this happens as a child, the wound can be difficult to heal. A child has no way to defend themselves from the conclusion that they are not worthy of being loved. They accept it and internalize it. As they get older, they bury it. If the wound happens when we are adults, from someone mistreating us or abandoning us, it often reopens old wounds of this sort.

The way to find healing is to forgive the person that hurt us. If we carry resentment and refuse to forgive, on some principle or as a defense mechanism, we only put a barrier between ourselves and the Lord. We become the wrongdoers by refusing to forgive. So much so that Jesus says, in Matthew 6:14-15, that our heavenly Father will not forgive us if we do not forgive those who have sinned against us. It doesn't seem fair, but this is how unforgiveness sits with God. It cannot be right to hold anything against someone if Jesus's death was necessary and sufficient to pay for what they did. We preempt God's right to cleanse people of their mistakes when we refuse to release them ourselves.

Offering forgiveness can be one of the hardest things we are called to do. The way to find the strength to do it is to realize that you have sinned also. If you have received God's forgiveness and know you are a flawed person in need of mercy, then you can choose to see others the same way. Jesus appeals to this in the case of the woman caught in adultery in John 8. We downplay adultery in our culture, but in his society, under the law, this was an act deserving of death. Jesus doesn't dispute the validity of that fact. He merely chooses to show the woman, and to all who gathered to render judgment, that any sin can be forgiven, and we have all failed in our own way. We want for ourselves what Jesus offered the woman— the chance for a fresh start if we will turn from our sins.

If you are carrying a burden from a wrong done to you, the Lord is asking you to set it down, like a stone that you hold in your hand. He is God and will make all things right. To release the burden you carry means that you trust him. You were the one inside the circle all along, with him standing at your side.

Divorce

There are many types of pain in divorce. There is the pain of being betrayed when a spouse leaves you. There is the disappointment of giving up on a marriage because you feel like, rightly or wrongly, you had no choice but to divorce your spouse. There is also the shame and anxiety that children feel when their parents get divorced because they cannot separate themselves from the reasons behind the tragedy. Even a person who leaves their marriage for no other reason than they find someone more attractive than their spouse will eventually manage the loss of the one-flesh relationship, though the preoccupation with an affair might hold the feelings off for a time. In the end, everyone coming through a divorce will experience some degree of damage.

If you feel betrayed, your pain is more immediate and acute. I have been in that position, and I have known many others—men and women who felt abandoned by someone they loved. I have also known and ministered to people who left their spouse and felt like their marriage couldn't continue for one reason or another. I'm not writing to cast blame or as part of a broader theological treatment of divorce. Nor am I writing to offer strategies to keep a marriage healthy and eliminate divorce as an option. These ideas are a book in themselves. I am writing for those who have experienced the pain of divorce in the hope they will find encouragement and hope in spite of it.

Husband and wife were intended to remain in a committed, exclusive relationship for life. God created us with that goal, that "a man leaves his father and mother and is united to his wife, and they become one flesh" (Gen. 2:24). *One flesh* expresses a relationship that is both sexual and spiritual. It is a connection between husband and wife—not only of bodies but souls. It is not intended to be broken (Mark 10:9). If it *is* broken by divorce or adultery, it tears the two apart. If two people are really one flesh, united not just physically but spiritually, then ripping them apart necessarily involves damage. The wound left behind isn't physical, though; it's within their souls.

We experience a high rate of divorce in today's world, and we live with the consequences. Marriage rates have been dropping for decades as fewer and fewer people want to expose themselves to the complications of divorce. We have broken families, a loss of self-esteem among children of divorce, and self-destructive behaviors. Divorce is at the center of all this, but it's wrong to look at it as the root cause and not a symptom of a bigger problem. It's not simply that we're choosing divorce but that we're getting married for the wrong reasons. We set ourselves up to fail from the outset. We create unhealthy marriages that have almost no chance to survive. Then, when things go wrong, we feel like we have no option but divorce. We might even reason, *God doesn't want me to be unhappy.* But the fact is that God wants us to be people who are close to him, who trust and follow him, and to marry others who do the same.

If you're someone from a failed marriage who wasn't the person you should have been, and you married someone who wasn't either, you might be living with the fallout of a divorce. If so, I have this insight: God has always wanted more for you than what you've settled for. Issues of sin in divorce or remarriage set aside, God wants you to become the person you are meant to be, and if you find someone who has a commitment to help you reach that goal, you have the basis for marriage as God intended. If you marry someone for any other reason, like mutual interests, physical attraction, or even a great sense of humor, it's the flip of a coin. Only fifty percent of marriages succeed in the United States. God doesn't merely want something more certain than fifty percent for us; he wants marriage to help us grow and reach our potential as his children. Marriage is meant to last a lifetime because it often takes that long to become the people we're meant to be. Marriage is intended to further that goal.

A relationship can propel us along our journey to become the people God intends for us to be, or it can stop us dead in our tracks. If you're divorced, you probably had an experience of the latter—that your marriage didn't bring you closer to God. You might even have been in a marriage that sent you in the opposite direction. But in the loss of that relationship, you have an opportunity to draw close to God. It's never a justification to pursue divorce—we are commanded to make marriage work, no matter how difficult. But if we are a casualty of a failed marriage, we need not give up hope. God can use the loss for our gain.

A failed relationship is like dealing with any other hardship, but in the case of divorce you learn something extra. God is enough for you. You don't need a person to fill your emptiness. Treating a relationship that way—as if it were intended to meet a need within us that only God can—is a recipe for disaster.

Relationships are not just neutral distractions; they influence us. If you choose someone who is headed on a path away from Jesus Christ, you are almost certainly going to be drawn that way also. If on the other hand, you marry someone who is in pursuit of Christ, you have the opportunity to share that journey with them.

This is at least part of the reason why Christians should not be "yoked" together with unbelievers (2 Cor 6:14). Husband and wife, like two oxen pulling a cart, won't make it far if they're heading in different directions. A lot of marriages are bad for precisely this reason. They go nowhere. Stuck in the mud of life's disappointments, they have no shared strength or vision. When difficulties hit, they have no common resource to draw upon. If you are the victim of divorce from this kind of relationship, you have a fresh opportunity to pursue Christ and allow the Spirit to guide you.

The pain of divorce is a wake-up call. If you've experienced it, it means you very likely weren't the person you should have been. But you can be the person God intends you to be *now*. Like any hardship, what you do with the disappointment is up to you. The world has a substitute for our pain. It provides its own options to supplant knowing Christ, and to make you feel better. Loneliness can control you if you allow it. Many people rush back into bad relationships when old ones fail. Don't forget the lesson we learned back in chapter 2: "As a dog returns to its vomit, so fools repeat their folly" (Proverbs 26:11). Hardship is a chance to halt the patterns that destroy our lives. Give yourself time to heal and allow the Lord to lead you to the life he has for you.

Chapter 8:
The Upward Calling

> *I want to know Christ—yes, to know the power of his resurrection and participation in his sufferings, becoming like him in his death, and so, somehow, attaining to the resurrection from the dead. (Phil. 3:10-11)*

Christianity is, at its core, a personal relationship with Jesus Christ. It's not just knowing something about Jesus; it's knowing him *personally*. Christians often explain their faith that way but don't always think through the implications. What does *knowing Jesus* really mean? What difference does it make, that we know him and not just know certain facts about him?

In today's world, we regard relationships as an opportunity for mutual affection, conversation, shared interests, and entertainment. Our friends are people we speak with often, have fun with occasionally, and like more than we dislike. We characterize relationships based on what they offer us, not what they cost us. We even approach marriage this way and talk about the need for our spouse to be a "best friend," overlooking the fact that we recycle friendships when they don't deliver everything we want. Many of our relationships do best when our primary point of contact is a text message, in fact. When we characterize our faith as a personal relationship with Jesus Christ, it becomes even less obvious what that means today than ever before.

For Paul, knowing Christ was the most important pursuit of his life. He walked away from physical comfort, the acclamation of his peers, and religious status to know Jesus. He not only took those steps, he also regarded them as essential. In other words, he viewed the relationship in terms of what it cost him, not what it delivered.

We find it difficult to view relationships that way because we've been taught that life is about getting and not giving. We've also been taught that relationships are based on the most superficial of connections, that a sense of humor and shared pastimes are more important than character, sacrifice, and selflessness. We use the same criteria for choosing people to marry, but still manage to be astonished when marriages fall apart, even between Christians.

For Paul, knowing Christ meant walking in his footsteps and sharing in his sufferings. It meant living the life of Jesus while he was on earth. When we participate in the work of Christ, we know him. Not in a superficial sense, but because we share the same life, the same values, and the same difficulties. We know him because we shoulder his burdens. It's the only meaningful way we know anyone in this life. We set aside our concerns and take on someone else's. Friendships and marriages built on sacrificial love and mutual regard are in rare supply, but they are the kind of relationships that last. At their core, they require proven character—the consequence of a life lived in pursuit of something greater than individual self-interest. These relationships are rare in a world of consumer values and selfish priorities.

In Philippians 3:10-11, Paul expresses knowing Christ in terms of *resurrection-power* and *suffering*. If you haven't skipped ahead to this part in the book, the combination of these two things will make perfect sense in light of the ground we've covered. They accompany one another. Jesus's resurrection-power isn't merely something that waits for you when you die; it's an experience of that power today. It's the power revealed by his resurrection, but available through the Spirit to those who know him. The way that you know him is by sharing in his sufferings. If you walk in his footsteps and maintain his values in today's world, you will suffer. Jesus predicted it (John

15:18-19; 16:33). It's a certainty. But so also is his power.

If we are in pursuit of the most comfortable life possible and follow our culture's dictates on how to achieve that life, we're not likely to see much of the power that Paul speaks of. Following Jesus doesn't necessarily mean we have to give up on a warm bed and three meals a day, but it does mean being willing to go wherever he calls us. It does mean trusting him and not relying on our strengths. It does mean being willing to set aside our dreams and share in his plans, whatever they might be and wherever they may take us.

It's not the version of Christianity that is peddled in Western culture, for the most part, but it is the version that leads to an experience of Jesus's power. Many are willing to live without that power, viewing the loss of their own hopes and dreams as too dear a cost. But the question is not merely whether we want to experience his power, but whether we want to know him. If I can convince you of just one thing, it is this: If you do come to know Jesus the way Paul describes, whatever you have lost along the way, it will be worth it.

Fixing Our Eyes on the Finish

And I heard a loud voice from the throne saying, "Look! God's dwelling place is now among the people, and he will dwell with them. They will be his people, and God himself will be with them and be their God. 'He will wipe every tear from their eyes. There will be no more death' or mourning or crying or pain, for the old order of things has passed away." (Rev 21:3-4)

Life can distract us with its demands, and particularly so if things are starting to take a bad turn. We end up trying to manage life to keep it from overwhelming us. It can be like a game of whack-a-mole, with one new crisis popping up as soon as we beat another down. Many consider retirement as the moment life will finally slow down and they'll get a chance to relax. What that often means is that the days leading up to that moment are lived in a frenzy. If life isn't complicated enough, we make it so. We come up with new crises and worries to fill our waking moments.

If we're distracted by the moment, we have a tendency to miss what lies ahead. We forget we're on a journey, bound for a destination beyond this life. We can overlook our purpose and spend our days focused on things that don't matter. When tragedy strikes, it's all the more horrible because it knocks us out of a routine. But it's often the very thing that causes up to stop, look up, and think about the finish line.

If we picture ourselves at the finish line, looking back at our lives, we can gain some insight about the difficulties we face today. From that vantage, we will almost certainly regard them in a different light. We might consider them unimportant, or at least, less important than they seemed at the time. We might view them in terms of the blessings that followed and less in light of what we lost. But one thing is certain—

we will view them with closure. There will be no sadness, no sense of disappointment, fear, pain, or heartache. Every wrong done to us will be made right, every loss replaced with the deepest joy and fulfillment. The cares and concerns we carried through life will be entirely gone.

There is nothing stopping you from placing yourself at that moment as you consider whatever you face, today. Paul lived in that moment and evaluated everything in his life from that perspective. His vision of the resurrected Christ on the road to Damascus was the dominating vision of his life. It drew him through extreme suffering and, in the end, death itself. Today, Paul stands with his Lord and Savior, in the place he pictured throughout his life and ministry. One day, you and I will join him there.

The way you catch that vision is by the power God reveals in your life today. Small measures of that same joy point to a final resolution that awaits you. As you have victory over one tragedy, you gain the courage to face another, and then finally, to leave this life behind altogether. Those who don't walk at least part way in Jesus's footsteps can't imagine how it will turn out, but the further you walk, the more real it will become. Discipleship is often that way, one step leading to another, with everything becoming clearer along the way, the closer you draw near to the end.

Jesus is calling you, today—telling you not to lose heart, whatever you face, but to trust him. To take one step after another, to lift your eyes from whatever is occupying you and look at what lies ahead. The path you're walking on leads directly to the one who loves you.

We Do Not Lose Heart

Therefore we do not lose heart. Though outwardly we are wasting away, yet inwardly we are being renewed day by day. For our light and momentary troubles are achieving for us an eternal glory that far outweighs them all. So we fix our eyes not on what is seen, but on what is unseen, since what is seen is temporary, but what is unseen is eternal. (2 Cor. 4:16-18)

In 2016, 44,965 people committed suicide. This makes suicide the tenth leading cause of death in the United States. Unsuccessful attempts to commit suicide are estimated at over twenty times this number. Men account for 80% of these deaths, and the highest rates in recent years have been tracked for men in the 45 to 54 age bracket.

There is a point in your life when despair sets in and you realize your dreams may never come true. For men, much of our identity revolves around accomplishment. The older we get, the more we realize that opportunities to reach our goals are running out. We fail at living up to the expectations we set for ourselves—the same expectations the world sets for a *successful* man. We are told that the measure of a man is his ability to provide for himself and his family. We cannot control the circumstances of life or most of our limitations as human beings. We are set up for failure from the outset.

Real life begins to take a toll in your fifties. Pushing through the loss of a job, a marriage, a home, a child—it's much easier when you're younger. There is always room to hope; time is on your side. As you grow older, you realize that your chances are largely behind you. Our past failures seem to control our thoughts; we live in the regret of missed opportunities and lost love. We are not the people we hoped to be. We cannot change the past.

I have reached points where I had no hope. I stood at one such point and realized I had thrown away opportunities for love and happiness at a time in my life filled with so many possibilities. I made poor choices, and in the end, lost almost everything that had become important to me. I had traded joy for something temporary. I've never thought about suicide, but I'd lost a sense of value for myself. There are other ways we hurt ourselves when we think so little of the life that remains.

Then I received an unexpected message from someone I'd known a long time ago. We hadn't communicated much over the years. I read it over and over.

> *I am so proud of you. It takes a great deal of courage to embark on a journey of self-discovery. . . God has always blessed you and challenged you at a higher level than the rest. No one achieves greatness without hardship. The worst has passed and you are still standing with God on your side. Well done, Mike.*

They weren't just her words to me, they were God's, at the moment I was desperate to hear them. I saw where I had taken a wrong turn in my thinking. The circumstances of life are outside our control, and to the degree we find our value in them, we are sure to lose heart. But our life is not about circumstances, it is about something inside us. Nothing can change the work God does in the hearts of men and women who serve him. Though outwardly we waste away, as Paul says in 2 Cor. 4:16, we are renewed deep in the core of who we are by a God who loves us more than anything, if we will only go his way and find our value in him. The path that Jesus took led to suffering and loss, but also the greatest fulfillment imaginable. We are called to follow him through the same hardships, and then onward to the same destiny.

Nothing can change the glory that awaits those who put their trust in him. Paul himself was beaten and persecuted, but he found his value in his Lord and Savior. It was because of that trust, and the all-surpassing power of God through him, that he was able to find joy and purpose in the middle of the worst situations of life. He goes so far as to call these "light and momentary troubles" (2 Cor. 4:17). They most certainly are, in light of eternity. The disappointments of this life will mean nothing on that day when we stand with Jesus. We must fix our eyes on that day, not on troubles that are temporary.

Satan seeks to rob us of our hope. It is easy to give in to it, to accept that we are failures by some worldly standard. I have bought into that lie myself. If you are

THREE TIMES I PLEADED

struggling, invest yourself in what cannot fail. Your value lies there. The measure of a man or a woman is found in a heart dedicated entirely to the Lord. Nothing in life can take that away.

Blessings Ahead

> *After Job had prayed for his friends, the Lord restored his fortunes and gave him twice as much as he had before. All his brothers and sisters and everyone who had known him before came and ate with him in his house. They comforted and consoled him over all the trouble the Lord had brought on him, and each one gave him a piece of silver and a gold ring. (Job 42:10-11)*

The story of Job is a behind-the-scenes look into the life of a man who experienced profound loss. Each time something was taken from him, Job refused to speak badly of God for permitting it. It is one of the greatest tests of faith imaginable, and one, I think, few people could have passed as successfully. Even Job's friends fail the test as they incorrectly guess at the reason for his suffering and assume God is punishing Job for his sin. In defense of Job's friends, we sometimes make similar misjudgments or even worse when things go wrong in our lives.

What is confusing about the story, though, is not why Job is picked to suffer—the story gives us at least a glimpse of the reason—but what God does at the conclusion of the matter. God gives Job greater wealth than he had originally. Job receives more children, even greater herds of livestock, and he lives to be older than anyone you've ever met. The temptation is to consider this a reward, which is almost the same mistake as regarding the test as a punishment in the first place. Job doesn't regain his fortune because he passed the test. If we think in those terms, both the test and the final outcome seem arbitrary— an unnecessary and even vain contest between God and Satan with a prize for playing along. Neither of those assumptions is true.

The story of Job frames the challenge facing all who intend to live a life of faith. This is not a unique, one-off contest. This is the purpose of all human life, from Eden to the return of Jesus Christ. It's the very question our lives are meant to answer: *Will we trust God when we face difficulties? Or will we turn from him and find a solution to our needs under our own power?* We're not all chosen to suffer like Job did, but we all face the same test. Jesus faced it and was victorious. Now, it's our turn.

Looked at in those terms, God doesn't bless Job because he passed the test. God blessed Job because he loved him. He restored Job's fortunes as an expression of his justice, out of compassion for Job's pain. Nothing can make up for the death of Job's children, of course. If the blessing were a reward, it would be a hollow mockery of Job's loss. It would limit the purpose of suffering to the test itself and not a transformation in the lives of those who persevere. Job's reward was not material wealth and prosperity; his reward was eternal. Ours is also.

As we face difficulties in life, we can be certain of God's love. As his children, we can depend on it no matter what life brings us. His faithfulness and compassion are new every morning. We can expect his blessings just as we can anticipate that circumstances won't always go our way. It's true whether we handle life's difficulties correctly or if we stumble from time to time. Our God brings restoration to those he loves—not because we are perfect people, but because he is our Father.

Keeping Faith

By faith Noah, when warned about things not yet seen, in holy fear built an ark to save his family. By his faith he condemned the world and became heir of the righteousness that is in keeping with faith. (Heb. 11:7)

The most difficult kind of faith is believing that everything will be right in the end, that God will reveal his goodness when things seem to be at their worst. If you've ever been in a spot where you've lost your job and you're facing the prospect of not being able to cover food and either rent or a mortgage, you know what I mean. Jesus's promise that our heavenly Father knows about our needs isn't much comfort when you are afraid, in a panic, and wondering what will happen next.

In these cases, your security has been ripped away from you, and you are dealing with pain, worry, and an uncertain future. You are left with one hope that, at the moment, seems only barely possible. One prayer.

Namely, that God will take care of you and, in the end, bless you beyond whatever you have lost, if you will simply trust and obey him.

I have been at low points and thought, *This is the worst thing I have ever gone through.* Then a number of years later, found myself thinking, *I was wrong, this is even worse.* And on and on. Each time, I had the choice to trust God or try to manage my way through it using my own strength. To put it in his hands or find another way to ease my pain and anxiety. If you go the latter route, you can end up in worse shape than when you started.

Noah—I don't have to say much about him because we all know the story. But imagine the laughing stock he was in his time. Building a huge barge, four stories tall, occupying the span of two football fields. He built it in the desert, 500 miles from the sea. He built it based on someone's promise, a word spoken to him. A word given to him by his God. That word was more real to him than the present reality because the one who gave it to him was trustworthy.

Noah trusted God because God had proven himself, over and over. The same way he later proved himself to Abraham, over and over. Each challenge in life, each step of faith, revealed more of God's love and faithfulness. If you trust him, the next time things go wrong, it is easier to believe he will come through. Eventually, you are a person of faith, like the people described in Hebrews 11.

God has never let me down. Not one time. The most important thing I can do, when my world is crumbling, is to look back at all the times he was faithful. The way he brought me through some of those times was difficult, but in the end, he was there, waiting for me. He was the light in the darkness (Isa. 42:16). All I had to do was continue walking toward him and not look back.

Follow his example. In the end, you, like Noah, will become an heir of the righteousness that comes by faith. God will not let you down. On the day that all this world offers is gone, he will be there waiting for you.

The Unfolding Vision

God's response to our faithfulness is an outworking of power for his purposes. Behind this is an idea that seems simple but might end up lost if we don't take note of it: God is in search of people that he can use for his glory. He takes note of those who yearn to know him and are willing to put their feet on his path. We live with the sense that our lives don't matter, that the moments we waste don't amount to much, and that our lives, overall, aren't very important. It's easy to waste an entire day watching television or playing video games if you don't think your life counts for much. We don't usually live with the sense that we have an audience, that both angelic and demonic beings are taking note of the decisions we make. If we did, we might make different choices. But the Bible confirms that reality.

In chapter 5, we looked at the prayer of Daniel (Dan. 9). Near the end of his life, Daniel is asking God to keep his promise to release Israel after seventy years in captivity, and he does so by taking responsibility for Israel's sin and acknowledging God's goodness and righteousness. As we noted, that prayer reflected the posture of a life of faith. What is most startling is not the prayer, though, but the answer he was given:

> *While I was speaking and praying, confessing my sin and the sin of my people Israel and making my request to the LORD my God for his holy hill—while I was still in prayer, Gabriel, the man I had seen in the earlier vision, came to me in swift flight about the time of the evening sacrifice. He instructed me and said to me, "Daniel, I have now come to give you insight and understanding. As soon as you began to pray, an answer was given, which I have come to tell you, for you are highly esteemed." (Dan. 9:20-23)*

Daniel not only receives an answer to his prayer but Gabriel, an angel, delivers the response in person. He not only tells Daniel that he has come to give him information about his request, but that the answer was on its way from the moment he began praying. In other words, God was listening and acted immediately.

We don't always have this vision that God is attentive to the needs and requests we bring to him, but that's because we don't pray the way Daniel did. We spend our prayers asking for things that almost always focus on something less than God's ideal, then react as if he wasn't listening anyway when we don't get what we want. We ask for *our* will to be done, not *his*. We don't approach prayer as a way to acknowledge our failure and ask God to do the thing that's in his plan, as Daniel did.

Those who pray for God's will to be done are *heard*. Their prayers are always answered. Those prayers are rare in a world of consumers, where everyone is taught they need just one more thing to be happy. In the case of Daniel, his prayer is heard precisely because he studied scripture and lined his request with something God intended to do anyway.

As we face difficulties, the temptation is to pray for a specific way of escape. But God knows our needs and has a solution in mind. Rather than ask for what we want, prayer is where we affirm his will. We ask him to reveal his purposes, to rescue us in his timing, and to change us. To glorify himself through our lives. That prayer will be answered. And you can be sure it will get his attention.

Gabriel tells Daniel that God is giving him an answer because he is "highly esteemed" (Dan. 9:23). Put yourself in his position for a moment. You have been praying, and an angel comes to you, in person, to give you the response you're looking for. And the angel tells you that the answer was dispatched because you are highly regarded in the heavenly places.

How does that make you feel, knowing they're talking about you in heaven? If you live a life of faith, the angels *are* watching and talking about you. When you forsake sin, walk away from your own plan, and invest your heart in God's plan, even the angels know and respond. The posture of your life matters on a level you cannot imagine. The reason Daniel finds himself the recipient of the vision that Gabriel came to offer him, and all the other amazing feats of miraculous power we read of in the book of Daniel, is because of the priorities in his life.

Daniel asks about the seventy years of Israel's captivity, but God's response is something far greater. He doesn't just give Daniel insight into the near future, but the far future. Daniel receives an outline of the end of the age, from the events leading up to the death of the Messiah to the second coming of Jesus Christ. Daniel asked about the seventy years, yearning for the fulfillment of God's promise. God told him about seventy times seven years, the 490 years that wrap up the fulfillment of every promise ever made to the Jewish people. Daniel asked about the restoration of Jerusalem, but God gave him a prophecy of the restoration of Israel in the coming kingdom.

In other words, God's response to Daniel's faithfulness is an outworking of power—arguably, the most important prophecy in the Bible framing the events around the return of Christ and the Messianic kingdom. It was greater than any answer Daniel could have imagined. God yearns for men and women who live like Daniel, who pray for his will and not their own. He is attentive to our requests in the middle of suffering, as we align our will with his and ask for his plans to unfold. He reveals his power in the lives of men and women who trust him and know him through the difficulties of life. He wants to reveal his power in your life too.

Chapter 9:
The Real Question

And the Lord said, "Listen to what the unjust judge says. And will not God bring about justice for his chosen ones, who cry out to him day and night? Will he keep putting them off? I tell you, he will see that they get justice, and quickly. However, when the Son of Man comes, will he find faith on the earth?" Luke 18:6-8

Few situations feel worse than being wronged by someone. It is the nature of all relationships—they have the power to heal and also to harm. Sometimes the people you love the most end up being the ones who hurt you. Sometimes it is the callous disregard of a stranger. We have no choice but to trust people, and that can result in harm to us. It's part of life.

I've been there a few times. I've cried out to God for justice over how I was being treated. I couldn't keep from thinking about it; I let myself be controlled by resentment. It's hard to hear God in those times, and if he doesn't step in to make things right, it's easy to grow bitter. I remember thinking, at one low point, *Why do I even bother to pray if you don't care about me, Lord?*

When prayers go unanswered, it's hard to envision that God may have his own timing about these things. In our pain, we may grow defensive and give up. We may doubt his goodness. Every day we go to him and he doesn't come through feels like more rejection.

We also live in a culture of immediate gratification. If we can't get what we want, the moment we want it, we lose patience and try something else. We treat God like he's Amazon.com—always available to provide exactly what we need at the moment we need it. If we can't get what we want, we assume it doesn't exist at all and try something different.

In Luke 18:1-8, Jesus tells a parable of a widow who nags a judge incessantly until he finally gives her the justice she asks for. He doesn't intend by this to suggest we can annoy God with our prayers to the point where he finally does what we ask. Our cries for justice don't irritate him, and he isn't going to do what he doesn't intend to, regardless. Jesus's point is that if even an unjust judge would do what is right purely to end the widow's appeals, how much more will our heavenly Father respond to the cries of the children he loves dearly?

The question isn't whether God loves us, or whether he will deliver justice and work all things out in his timing. He does, and he will. The real question is whether we will be faithful as we wait for him to do so.

The only way we can show God we trust him is by actually doing it. It's all fine to say we have faith, but in the end, faith is not a profession from our lips but the response of our lives. Trust means being willing to wait. It means placing our cares into his hands and following him, no matter what. We may not see justice, and when it comes, it may not be what we expect. It may take a long time. If we trust God, though, we know that he loves us and will not let injustice stand. He will defend his chosen ones. The injustice we experience in our lives and the injustice that thrives on the earth will all ultimately be put to rest.

Trusting him means forgiving what has been done to us. It means releasing bitterness and returning mistreatment with love. It means obeying him and not finding a quick way out of our pain. It means being willing to pray as long as it takes, to show him we submit to his timing and agree in our hearts with his purposes.

When the Son of Man comes back, will he find faith on the earth? That's the real question. Jesus doesn't sound as hopeful in Luke 18:8 as we might expect. An even bigger question presents itself. *Will he find faith in me?* This is the only question I can answer. It is the question you can answer for yourself, as well. Trust the Lord with your life. He will make all things right. Obey him as you wait patiently for that day.

Appendix

Christianity isn't a religion, at its core; it's an account of how the Creator of the universe made it possible for you to share his life. Christianity spells out the means by which you receive that life and draw near to him. All people have been created in his image, but by their moral failure have separated themselves from the Creator. His perfect nature cannot be connected to moral failure, nor can his life reside in an imperfect vessel. As much as he loves us and wants to give us his life and draw near to us, his perfection won't permit it.

The resolution to our problem is found in the Creator himself. He entered into time and space by becoming a man, and through an act of sacrificial love, offered his life in our place, imputing his moral perfection to us while taking the burden of our failure upon himself. The offering of his own morally perfect human life on our behalf was sufficient to satisfy God's perfect justice.

Through an act of trust, we can set aside our flawed lives and receive his perfect life. If we do, we become part of the same family—sons and daughters of a Heavenly Father—and share the destiny of the one who loved us and died for us. Christianity is about that and nothing else—the sacrificial death of Jesus Christ at a point in human history, to the goal of offering you spiritual life—his life—and a relationship with the God who created you. The life he offers you is the life you were created to have. It begins immediately and continues even when biological life ends. It's available to you right now.

To receive it and draw into a relationship with him, you have to trust him enough to give him your old life. In exchange, he gives you his, and all that implies. You can receive it by praying a prayer like this one:

Lord, I have made mistakes. I have crossed lines I should not have. I have trusted myself instead of trusting you. I have hurt others and hurt myself. I acknowledge I am not the person I should be or the person you created me to be. But I want to be that person, and I want to know you.

Jesus, I acknowledge that you are the one true God and Savior. I accept your death on the cross on my behalf, two thousand years ago, as an expression of your love for me. I ask that your blood wash me clean of my mistakes and failures. I accept your love and forgiveness. I ask that you give me your life and take my old one.

In receiving your life, I commit to living for you. Give me a new heart and guide me to the kind of life you want for me. Set me free from the lies I have believed and the things which I have allowed to control me. Show me how to trust you completely.

Study Questions

Introduction: Crossroads of Decision

1. Make a list of all the difficult life situations you are facing, big or small. Include in the list things that cause you frustration, pain, and anxiety. Rate each one on a scale of one to ten, where *one* indicates it bothers you a little and occasionally forces its way into your thinking, and *ten* indicates you can barely stop thinking or worrying about it.

2. Considering the items in your list, what is your biggest fear, at the moment? What would happen if circumstances don't go the way you hope? What do you stand to lose?

3. Is there anything about what you're facing or feeling that would be difficult for others to understand? If so, what is it? Why does it have such a strong influence on you?

4. For each item in your list, write one sentence about how you can trust God with the situation you're facing. If you had confidence God was in total control, would your feelings about that situation change?

5. Read 2 Cor. 11:24-30. What encouragement or insight can you draw from reading Paul's list?

Chapter 1: A Shift in Perspective

1. Hollywood invents its own picture of happiness through the movies and programs it creates. Share or write down one of those images that comes to mind. Why were the people in the story happy?

2. Make a list of the possessions and pursuits that are important to you. (*Possessions* are objects that have intrinsic value to you, like a car, golf clubs, or jewelry. *Pursuits* are things you invest your time in, like hobbies or your career. The list should include things like happy hour, time spent in relationships, and any medication you're taking. It's okay if your list is long.) Now, scratch out the items in your list that will still be important after you die. For the rest, rate each from one to ten. *One* means it has a small influence on your time, money, and thoughts. *Ten* means it is very important and you're never giving it up!

3. Read Matt. 6:19-21. One day you will be forced to give up everything in your list—some sooner than later. Generally speaking, what can you do to make the items in your list less important? If you did, what result would that have on your life?

4. Have you prayed a prayer and not received what you've asked for? What was it? Does prayer work, in your experience? What causes you to pray? If things are going wrong, are you more or less likely to pray? In those situations,

do you feel like you're more or less likely to get the answer you're looking for?

5. Read Rom. 12:1-2. In v. 1, Paul urges us to adopt a certain kind of behavior. If we do, it leads to the result in v. 2, which expresses a change in the way we think. What are some of the things that might change, as he describes in v. 2, if you did what he says in v. 1? What patterns of thought have you adopted from the world you live in that might not be helping you? What patterns of behavior lie behind those thoughts?

Chapter 2: Purpose in Suffering

1. Read John 1:5; 8:12. These verses remind us of an important idea: We are surrounded by darkness, just as Jesus was when he was on earth, but this doesn't mean darkness is winning. Does this change the way you think of the difficulties you're facing? What does God want you to remember?

2. Read Ps. 22:1-2. Is it okay to tell God he seems far away when things are going wrong? Does he want you to be real when you come to him in prayer? Why or why not?

3. Read Rom. 8:17. What does Paul mean, we are co-heirs with Christ "if indeed we share in his sufferings"? How does suffering show we are children of God? Have you had an experience where someone has shared in your suffering?

4. Read Eph. 6:10-17. This passage implies Satan is involved in an attack on God's children. If you picture yourself girding for battle, as Paul describes, what does that look like for you, practically speaking? How do you prepare for an attack from ideas and situations leveled against you, as God's child? Where are you most vulnerable to attack?

5. Make a list of at least three offensive and defensive strategies as you prepare for battle. For example: List the best defense to stop _____ (fill in the blank with something that has the potential to take you down). List the best offense to _____ (fill in the blank with something you can do to further God's purposes and have victory).

6. Read Rom. 8:20-21. When human beings turned away from God, the world became a dangerous place. But God has a plan for the creation that is tied to the fate of human beings. What does this tell us about the difficulties we face and how God feels about them? Does this explain why he doesn't just remove disaster and disease if he could?

7. Go back to the list of difficulties you made (question 1 in the *introduction* section, above). How many of those difficulties are the direct result of choices you made? Do you regard these differently than problems you were not directly responsible for? Do they

have a stronger or weaker influence over you, as a result?

Chapter 3: The Case for Weakness

1. Read Rom. 8:22-23. Not all pain is the same. If we think of this broken and dark world as if it's locked in childbirth, what picture does that paint of the future? If you think of the difficulties you face the same way, how does that cause you to reenvision the pain you're dealing with?

2. Go back and read the list of difficulties you made (question 1 in the *introduction* section, above). Picture yourself as someone who has come through these things victoriously and brought glory to God. How is that person different than the person you are today? How could God change you and do something positive in your life through the items on your list?

3. Read 2 Cor. 12:7-10. Why does God refuse to remove Paul's suffering? Why does Paul come to accept and rejoice in his weaknesses? Is this the picture most people have of the Christian life? Why or why not?

4. Read 1 Cor. 1:27-29. Why is this good news? List the top three weaknesses you have, and in each case, think of a way that God could use your weakness and work through you to reveal his power and presence to others.

5. In 2 Cor. 4:7, Paul talks about the treasure we have inside ourselves. Most treasures we see are locked up in a fancy museum. If you put a treasure in a jar of common clay, what would that communicate about the treasure? If people saw you that way, like a jar of clay in which the power of God was revealed, how could God use you for his glory?

6. Read 2 Cor. 4:8-12. This is part of what it means to be a jar of clay. How do difficulties make it easier for people to see God in our lives? Why doesn't it always work out this way, when we face hardships?

Chapter 4: Pride and Consequences

1. Nebuchadnezzar, the king of Babylon, is a clear example of pride because he makes no effort to disguise it. But the dimensions of his pride—thinking everything is about him, and that he's entitled to do whatever he wants—are powerful ideas in the world today. Why are we taught that focusing on ourselves is a good thing?

2. Read Prov. 12:15; 19:20-21; 21:24; 28:26. The Bible is loaded with wisdom on taking advice. Pride leads us to do what we think is right in our own minds. How approachable are you when you have your mind set on a course of action? Who has the right to call you on the decisions you're making if they're taking you in the wrong direction?

3. In the United States, the Declaration of Independence states that we have life, liberty, and the pursuit of happiness as inalienable rights. The way this is often interpreted in today's world is that we have the right to do anything we want. Read Prov. 16:18. Do you have examples of times you did whatever you wanted but ended up trapped by circumstances and in trouble?

4. Read Dan. 4:34; Luke 15:17-20. There often comes a moment when our selfish plans fail and we come to our senses. It sometimes takes difficulties to cause us to regard our priorities differently and return to God. Have you had a moment like that? How did God reach you, and what changes did you make afterward?

5. Read Prov. 13:14, 24; Ps. 23:4. The rod is a symbol of discipline—not for arbitrary punishment but a tool for guidance. The difficulties we face in life, however extreme, are welcome if they keep us from walking down a path to destruction. Have you walked through the valley that David writes about in Ps. 23:4? If so, did you face hardships that kept you from something even worse?

Chapter 5: Sovereign Over All

1. Read Jonah 1:1-3. What are some of the ways you run from the Lord? What does he want from you that is so difficult? Why do we think

we'll get away? God sent a fish to swallow Jonah. Have you ever felt like circumstances overcame you, leaving you trapped and powerless? How did you react?

2. Read Jonah 2:1. What was the turning point for Jonah? Why do you think it took so long for him to pray? How long would it take you, trapped inside a giant fish, before you started praying? How long does it take you, when you face hardships, before you finally start to pray? Is this the way you think of prayer—as a way to adjust your thinking and agree with God's plans?

3. Read Jonah 2:8-9. Jonah says he will sacrifice to God with "shouts of grateful praise." Why have his circumstances led to thankfulness? Jonah says that those who worship idols separate themselves from God's love. How is running from God and ignoring his will a kind of idolatry? Have you experienced God's love when you turned to him in the middle of hardship?

4. Read Daniel 9:1-14. Make a list of God's characteristics, as identified by Daniel, and Israel's. Daniel has a list in mind of Israel's mistakes. Why is taking stock of your mistakes helpful when things go wrong in your life? Why is it difficult for us, especially in today's world, to take responsibility for our failure?

5. As you look over the list of Israel's mistakes in Dan. 9, check off the ones you've made in

your own life. How did you feel about your mistakes, at the time? How do you feel about them now? What did God teach you?

6. Read Rom. 8:31-32. These are rhetorical questions. What is the answer, in each case? If this is true, why do we worry about the future?

7. Read John 14:27. Jesus knows that life is full of difficulties and that it's difficult not to be afraid. His solution is to give us his peace. How is Jesus's peace—the peace that allowed him to remain obedient to death on the cross—the thing we need the most in today's world?

Chapter 6: Power Made Perfect

1. Read Gal. 5:22-24. For each characteristics of the Spirit-controlled life, indicate whether you experience it more when life is *good* or more when life is *difficult*:

    Love _____

    Joy _____

    Peace _____

    Forbearance (patience) _____

    Kindness _____

    Goodness _____

    Faithfulness _____

    Gentleness _____

    Self-control _____

2. Read Phil. 2:5-11. In v. 7, Paul says that Jesus "made himself nothing" (NIV), but the words

literally mean he *emptied himself*. This is the concept behind humility that Paul practiced (see Phil. 3:7-8). Why is it so hard to empty our lives of things, in our culture today? Refer back to your list of possessions and pursuits (*chapter 1*, question 2, above). Go through the list and consider whether each item is standing in the way of God filling you with his power and presence. Paul said he considered the items on his list "rubbish." Submit each item to God in prayer and ask him to change your heart if it's interfering with his purposes in your life. If so, write "rubbish" next to it.

3. In John 14:12, Jesus said that whoever believes in him will do greater things than he did. As we look around, in Western culture, we don't see many miracles happening. (Or, to the degree they are happening, they're not visible to most of us.) Read Matt. 17:20. What prevents God from working powerfully? Why are we not experiencing the kind of faith that leads to God's power? Does God want to reveal his power in our lives? How do you want to see his power revealed in your life?

4. Read Phil. 4:11-13. Paul talks about a secret he learned, how to be content in any and every situation. He specifically names the secret in v. 13. It's the same secret he speaks of in 2 Cor. 12:10. How did Paul learn the secret? We sometimes use Phil. 4:13 as a life verse, but it's only true if we approach difficulties a

certain way. How should you approach circumstances, whether good or bad, to realize God's power in your life? Why is it hard to accept that God is enough?

Chapter 7: Deep Wounds

1. Read John 11:25-26. Jesus's solution to Martha's pain is to draw her attention from circumstances to him. What truth is Jesus trying to reveal through the death of her brother? If this is the greatest form of hardship we face in life, what does this tell us?

2. Jesus claims to be the resurrection and the life. He is the answer to all our questions about pain and suffering. As the *resurrection*, he is the resolution to the worst that life can throw at us—the victory we have over death. As the *life*, he is the power that we have today, to prepare us in advance for the difficulties that lie ahead and to carry us through them. Refer back to the list of problems you are facing (*introduction*, question 1, above). How does Jesus, as the resurrection and the life, offer you what you need to face each item on your list?

3. When someone hurts us, we have the temptation to let circumstances lead us away from the direction the Spirit is guiding us. Our flesh can take over. Read Gal. 5:20. Complete a sentence for each of these, keeping in mind how you feel when you're hurting:

I reject hatred because _____

I reject discord because _____

I reject jealousy because _____

I reject fits of rage because _____

I reject selfish ambition because _____

I reject dissensions because _____

I reject factions because _____

I reject envy because _____

I reject drunkenness because _____

4. Read John 8:1-11. This is an emotionally-charged situation, and while we normally empathize with the woman (because Jesus is standing with her) we can also imagine her husband's pain over her betrayal. What Jesus causes us to see is that we are all on the inside of the circle, in need of forgiveness for our mistakes. Has someone hurt you in the past? Are you carrying a stone you need to lay down? What does God need to do so that you can scratch that hurt off your list of difficult life situations?

5. Read John 4:15-18. When the Samaritan woman at the well asks Jesus for a drink of the living water, Jesus asks her a question and exposes her past—that she has been married five times, and is now in an unmarried relationship. God hates divorce (Mal. 2:16), but this doesn't stop Jesus from offering this woman the life she needs. Her past, in fact, exposes her need. This episode and John 8 show that the power of God is greater than

our failures or our tragedy. Read Eph. 1:18-21. How does our identity in Christ overshadow our accomplishments and our failures, the worst things we've done as well as the worst things others have done to us?

Chapter 8: The Upward Calling

1. Read Phil. 3:10-11. Paul charts a path in the Christian life through suffering and power, leading to a destiny where we will one day share Jesus's resurrection. The life we live and the destiny that lies ahead are connected. This is what it means to know Christ, according to Paul—to experience the power of his resurrection and participation in his sufferings. Do you know Jesus this way? What stands in the way?

2. Read Rev. 21:3-5. John is given a glimpse of a moment when God will remove all evil, pain, and suffering from the world. Picture being present, together with Jesus, when that happens. How will you feel then, looking back on the items on your list of difficulties and struggles? Why is it difficult to keep that vision in front of you?

3. Read 2 Cor. 4:16-18. It's easier to focus on things that are tangible, in the here-and-now, than on a future under God's control. How does the world make it hard for you to stay focused? What can you do, practically speaking, to keep your eyes fixed on the goal?

4. Read Dan. 9:20-23. What does this tell you about God's opinion of prayer, when we use it to affirm his will and not our own? What do Gabriel's words reveal about the importance of how we live our lives?

Chapter 9: The Real Question

1. Read Luke 18:1-8. Jesus tells a parable to show the disciples they should continually pray and not give up just because they don't get a response right away. Even an unjust judge will eventually do the right thing, but in the case of a righteous and loving God, it's even more the case. What does this teach you about seeking God in the middle of difficult times? Why shouldn't we doubt his goodness even if we are not rescued right away? Do you have a tendency to give up on God when he doesn't answer the way you want?

2. In v. 8, Jesus puts himself into the conclusion to the parable. He is the Son of Man, and one day he will return to make everything right. It's a promise we can count on. It's certain. What's not certain is how many of us will be here, waiting faithfully and patiently for him in a dark and oppressive world, when he comes. That's the real question: "However, when the Son of Man comes, will he find faith on the earth?" How will you answer that, with regard to your own life? What will that faith look like?

About the Author

Michael Cranford is a writer and speaker whose heart is centered on equipping others to face the challenges of following Christ in today's world.

He was for eight years a professor of biblical studies at Biola University and Talbot School of Theology, located in La Mirada, California. He holds a B.A. in Philosophy from the University of California at Irvine, a Master of Divinity from Talbot School of Theology, and an M.A. and Ph.D. in Religion and Social Ethics from the University of Southern California.

Michael is also a software architect, a pioneer in video game development dating back to the eighties, and a web application developer with a current focus on voice recognition and artificial intelligence. He brings together an understanding of Christianity, social ethics, and our modern technological society to offer a practical and devotional strategy for the Christian life that makes sense of the world we live in.

He has been published in such diverse journals as *New Testament Studies, The Journal of Business Ethics,*

Technology in Society, and *Novum Testamentum.*

Michael has three children – Logan, Leilani, and Dylan – and Sean, a stepson. He lives in Southern California.

http://OneSteadfast.com
https://facebook.com/OneSteadfast
https://twitter.com/OneSteadfast
http://en.wikipedia.org/wiki/Michael_Cranford

.